Accounting

Reference #200

Recording Transactions Using Debits & Credits

By

Robert

Bob Steele CPA

http://accountinginstruction.info/

http://www.youtube.com/c/AccountingInstructionHelpHowToBobSteele

http://bobsteelecpa.com/

Contents

Ch. 1 Overview

This book covers the heart of financial accounting, the building blocks of financial accounting, and the practical skills of recording transactions needed to build financial statements and understand how financial statements are built.

Although it is possible to read financial statements without a full understanding of how they are constructed, and it is possible to work in an accounting department performing accounting tasks including data entry, without fully understanding debits and credits, it is not possible to have a complete understanding of the financial statements or financial accounting without an understanding of transactions recorded using debits and credits. An understanding of how the system works is what provides an individual real value in today's marketplace because it is understanding that is needed to fix problems and know when there are problems that need to be fixed.

Financial transactions recorded using debits and credits are the foundation for advanced financial accounting topics, a better understanding of debits and credits making advanced topics much easier to absorb.

The best way to learn how to record transactions using debits and credits is by doing, by working practical examples. This book will provide many practical examples and will provide links to free resources offering more examples and explanations including instructional videos, games, and discussion forums.

Before we jump into recording transactions we will cover a process for thinking about debits and credits, starting with a definition of debits and credits, followed by a systematic way to think through the recording of transactions. We will consider each account type including, assets, liabilities, equity, income, and expense accounts and discuss their normal balances, whether they have a debit or credit normal balance. We will start our recording of journal entries with those related to cash because they are the easiest to understand. We will then record transactions by cycle, commencing with the sales cycle and then the purchasing cycles. We will then include a comprehensive problem, recording transactions by date, posting transactions to the general ledger, and constructing a trial balance from the general ledger.

Our previous book, Accounting Instruction Reference #100, is recommended before advancing to this book but is not required. Accounting Instruction Reference #100 analyzes accounting transactions using the accounting equation and covers fundamental accounting terms and concepts.

Ch. 2 Review of Our Accounting Approach and The Accounting Equation

Let's start playing the game, start recording transactions and use them to make financial statements!

We promise that we will get to the exciting process of recording transactions in this text, but like anything worth learning, including games, music, or puzzles, we must first learn a few ground rules so that we know how the game works.

As we move forward, learning more accounting concepts, it's important to keep the end goal of financial accounting in mind, to keep our end users in mind. Financial accounting is aimed at external users like investors, creditors, government, and customers. Financial statements are the end product produced by financial accounting and used by external users to make investing decisions, financing decisions, determine if a company follows laws and regulations, and decide if they want to do business with a company.

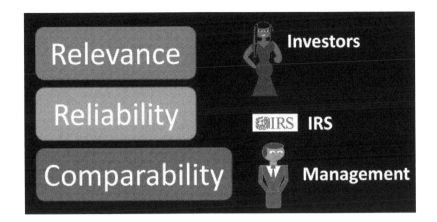

Click for Video

We focused on generating transactions using the accounting equation in our prior book, Accounting Instruction Reference #100, and emphasized the value of thinking of accounting as a kind of game, a sort of puzzle, and something to figure out. Keep this fun factor in mind as we learn debits and credits because thinking of these new concepts as a kind of game will make the process more fun and easier to understand. Like any game, we must start out by learning the rules, and memorizing a bunch of rules is not the fun part of any game, but once rules have been learned, playing the game provides greater enjoyment.

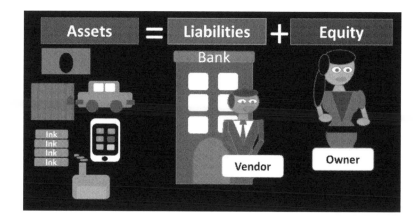

Click for video

Learning debits and credits can be compared to playing a game of Tic Tac Toe. Although Tic Tac Toe is a simple game it still requires rules to play, rules that need to be memorized before moving forward with the enjoyment of playing the game, rules like learning how to set up the table, knowing who goes first, and understanding how the game is won?

The simplicity of Tic Tac Toe allows for the rules to be learned relatively quickly and therefore the enjoyment of the game can be achieved quickly. However, the simplicity of the game also means that the amount of enjoyment that can be derived from learning the game is limited, the mastery of the game being possible in a relatively short period of time, resulting in every match ending with a tie. More complex games, like checkers or chess, are harder to learn but once learned have the potential to provide long-lasting enjoyment.

The Tick Tack Toe board is set up as a kind of grid, a nice little spreadsheet. Accounting can be thought of as being set up in much the same way, the board being a T-account or ledger. The rules of Tick Tack Toe provide guidance on where to put the Xs and Os. The rules of accounting will give guidance on where to put debits and credits, which side of the T-account the debits and credits should fall. Like checkers or chess, accounting is a more complex game than Tick Tack Toe, but can also provide more satisfaction and be directly applicable to practical applications.

People are often concerned about the complexity of math involved in accounting, imagining the math to be very complex, or that accounting itself is some unique form of math. Learning accounting

principles can be challenging, but it is not math complexity that provides

the biggest challenge, the biggest challenge being the learning and

memorization of the rules of the game, the rules of the double entry

accounting system. There are many areas of accounting and related

fields that utilize complex mathematics, so if math is something you are

passionate about you can find a fulfilling career in an accounting related

field, but core concepts guiding financial accounting do not require

complicated math. Financial accounting will start off with basic

mathematical operations, and students usually have access to a

calculator or computer.

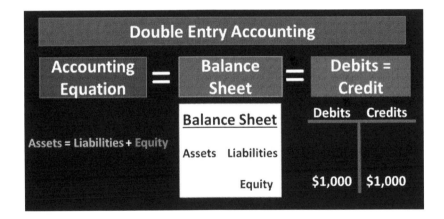

There are many ways the double entry accounting system can

be expressed including the use of an accounting equation, debits and

credits, and the balance sheet. It's important to know all three ways to

express the accounting equation because this allows us to better communicate with different people, people who have experience in various areas of business. For example, people working in public accounting will often talk in terms of debits and credits, debits and credits being the building blocks of the financial statements, similar to the bricks that make up a building. The job of public accounting is to make sure these bricks, these debits and credits, are lined up correctly, so that the financial statements are presented properly. Creditors, banks, and investors will not generally speak in terms of debits and credits, however. Their preferred way of referring to the double entry accounting system is the financial statements, the balance sheet representing the double entry accounting equation. Creditors, banks, and investors are less concerned with debits and credits in a similar way that a real estate agent is less focused on the bricks within the wall then on how the wall looks to potential buyers. As accountants, we will focus on the building blocks of the financial statement, on debits and credits.

In this book, we will focus primarily on debits and credits, the fundamental building blocks of financial accounting, and the most important concept to understanding how financial data is processed, stored, and made into financial statements. Debits are credits are fundamental financial accounting concepts and must be understood to move forward. Understanding debits and credits does not mean that a student must be able to record every transaction perfectly to proceed but does mean that a student needs to have a good foundation of the rules behind debits and credits to understand financial accounting concepts. Time reviewing debits and credits is always time well spent just like practicing the fundamentals is always necessary to learn a new sport like a baseball. Learning advanced aspects in the sport of baseball will improve performance, but we should spend a substantial part of every practice playing catch, swinging the bat, and digging up ground balls. Practicing debits and credits is like playing catch, and should be part of every accounting practice.

Ch. 3 Debits and Credits Defined

Although learning how debits and credits work is not an easy process, learning the definitions of debits and credits is and easy process. Debit can be defined as "recorded on the left side" (John J. Wild, 2015) and credit can be defined as "recorded on the right side" (John J. Wild, 2015). Note that these are partial definitions of debits and credits from the text, Fundamentals Accounting Principles, Wild 22nd, but they are the important parts, the parts that define what debits and credits are, the rest of the definition explaining what debits and credits do.

The definition of debits as, recorded on the left, and credits as, recorded on the right, implies something to be recorded on like, a board, paper, account, or ledger. A T-account can be imagined as the board, or ledger, used to record debits and credits. The debits are recorded on the left. The credits are recorded on the right.

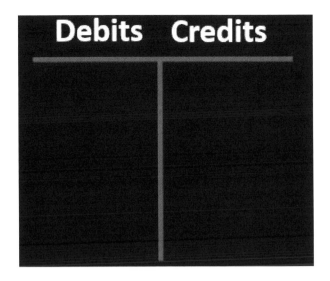

When thinking about debits and credits in the context of financial transactions, entering financial data, and creating financial statements, the definition above is the only definition we should have in mind. It is difficult to limit our thoughts and definition of debits and credits to the amount recorded on the left or right side of a T-account, or ledger, reducing all notions of debits and credits to no more placeholders, similar to the black and red pieces on the checkerboard. The black and red pieces on a checkerboard have no real meaning, the pieces in no way holding the rules, or idea, of the game of checkers, but when we see checker pieces we think of much more than black and red placeholders. We think of the game and how it works.

The same is true when we hear the terms, debit and credit, the terms often having a meaning to us that is so much more than the placeholders they actually are. The difference between how the concepts of debits and credits relate to accounting and how the concepts of checker pieces relate to the game of checkers, is that most of us learned how to play the game of checkers while also learning the definition of what checker pieces are, but most of us have not fully learned the game of accounting. Although we have heard the terms of the accounting pieces used in many different contexts, the accounting pieces being debits and credits, we have not learned these terms in relation to generating financial statements. The fact that we have learned definitions related to debits and credits apart, or outside of, the accounting game leads to false, or incomplete, understandings of what the words mean.

When learning how to record accounting transactions, we need to get back to the core definitions, requiring us first to unlearn definitions we may have picked up in our lives, meanings which may not be complete. These definitions can be revisited and understood from a new perspective once we know how debits and credits are used to record transactions.

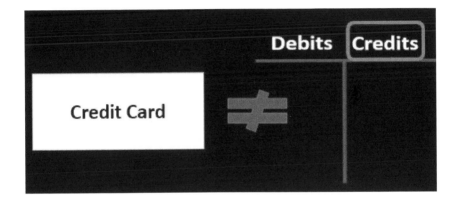

Click for video

Examples of the term credit being used in a misleading, or incomplete, ways are when we think about credit cards, credit terms, or a bank increasing our account with a credit. These uses of the phrase credit are derived from the original meaning of the word, the definition of the amount on the right side, but have come to mean different things to different people. After we learn accounting transactions and see how debits and credits are used in them, we should revisit these terms to understand the origin and evolution of their meaning in different contexts.

An example of how life experiences can lead to an incomplete understanding the terms debit and credit is a bank agreeing to eliminate a charge on a customer's balance by saying they will credit the customer's account. This transaction causes the customer to think of the term credit as a good thing, an increase in their checking account balance. While the credit does represent an increase to the client balance, the accounting definition of credit is an amount reported on the right side of a T-account or ledger, the bank reporting an amount on the right side of their ledger. When we see the bank statement, we see the bank recording credits as an increase to our account balance but from the bank perspective increases to our account balance are not assets but liabilities, amounts representing the bank owing money to the customers.

Using the definition of debits and credits as just amounts recorded on the left and right side of a T account, or ledger, is another area we ask learners to have faith in the system, to trust that these simple definitions are correct. Having patience and holding back on spending too much time analyzing other preconceived definitions of debits and credits until after we have learned how to record transactions often helps prevent these preconceived definitions from slowing down the learning process. Once we understand the accounting game and how debits and credits are used to play it, we will be better equipped to fully understand any definitions we previously had about debits and credits and analyze how they line up, and or fit within, the

definition of debits and credits.

Ch. 4 Account Types & Normal Balances

We have referred to a T-account or ledger multiple times, comparing it to a checkerboard, the T-account or ledger being where we line up the accounting pieces of debits and credits. At its most basic level, we can think of the accounting board as a T, debits lining up on the left side and credits lining up on the right side.

Setting up the accounting board is more like a game of chess than a game of checkers because we need to understand where each piece lines up on the board; we need to know each account's normal balance. We can group each account into account types of assets, liabilities, equity, revenue, and expense. We then need to know each account types normal balance, whether the account lines up on the debit or credit side of the T-account, or ledger, accounts lining up on the left having a normal balance of a debit, accounts lining up on the right having a normal balance of a credit.

Below is a table showing the normal balances for the account types. We recommend keeping a table like this with you as much as possible because it is a good reminder, a guide, and a cheat sheet.

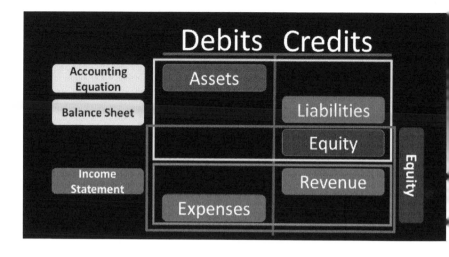

At this point we may be thinking, this looks like a lot of information to memorize, but hang in there. Learning the account types on the board above, and where they line up on the board, the T or ledger, is less memorization then we need to learn when playing many kinds of games, and we can usually have a reminder, a cheat sheet, like the one above, with us until it becomes natural.

As we can see from the cheat sheet the normal balances or the balances where each account type lines up are:

- **Assets** have a normal balance of a debit because they line up on the left side, or debit side, of the T-account, or ledger.

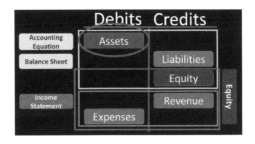

- **Liabilities** have a normal balance of a credit because they line up on the right side, or credit side of the T-account, or ledger.

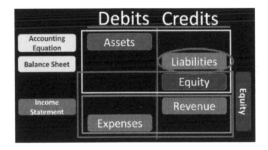

- **Equity**, as a total, usually has a normal balance of a credit because they line up on the right side, or credit side of the T – Account, or ledger. The equity account can be confusing because it can include temporary accounts but, for now, remember that total equity usually has a credit balance.

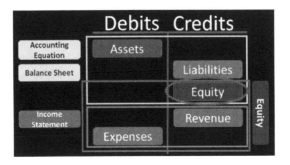

- **Revenue** accounts have normal credit balance because they line up on the right side, or credit side of the T-account, or ledger.

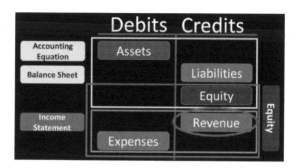

- **Expense** accounts have a normal debit balance because they line up on the left side, or debit side of the T-account, or ledger.

Ch. 5 Definition of Account Types & List Accounts Per Account Type

Now that we have an idea of where each account type lines up on the T-account, or board, or at least have a cheat sheet to help us line up the account types on a T-account, or board, we will review the definition of each account type and list some accounts that fall into each account type category.

Assets	Liabilities	Equity
• Cash	• Account Payable	• Capital
• Account Receivable	• Notes Payable	• Draws
• Equipment		• Income
		• Expense

Assets are resources owned by the business. The most common asset is cash, but assets also include accounts receivable, prepayments, land, building, and equipment. Assets are items that have not yet been consumed, resources planned to be used in the future to achieve business goals, to help generate revenue.

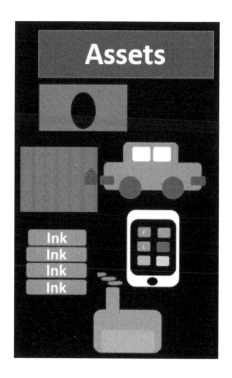

Liabilities are claims by creditors. Liabilities come about from a transaction that happens in the past that obligates the company for some form of future payment. Purchasing something on a credit card is an example of how a liability can be created, the transaction creating a future obligation to pay cash. Liability accounts include accounts payable, notes payable, and bonds payable.

Equity is the owner's claim to assets. Equity is equal to assets minus liabilities. Equity is often the most confusing section of the accounting equation, in part, because different organization types will organize the equity section differently and because the equity section is involved in the closing process of temporary accounts.

The equity section represents what is owed to the owner on a book basis. This is best illustrated by imagining we liquidate, or close, a business, selling the assets for cash, and then paying off the liabilities. The money left over would be equal to the equity section if all sales were made on a book value basis.

The equity section for a sole proprietor will be called owner's equity and consist of one capital account. The equity section of a partnership will be called partner's equity and include two or more owners, and therefore, two or more capital accounts. The equity section of a corporation will be called shareholder's equity, shareholders being the owners of a corporation, and will include capital stock and retained earnings. Although the format changes, the equity section, taken as a whole, can still be thought of as what is owed to the owner, or owners in, each case.

When thinking about the accounting equation, the equity section includes all temporary accounts, including revenue accounts and expense accounts.

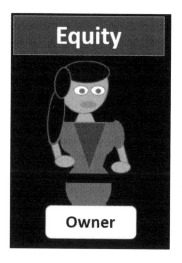

Revenue - is income generated from performing work. Revenue is not the same thing as cash. Cash is a form of payment while revenue represents the creation of value, the earning of compensation. Revenue is a timing account, needing to be measured over a time frame, a starting and ending point. For example, when somebody says they earn $100,000, the concept has no meaning unless we assign a time frame, most people naturally attributing a year as the time frame when hearing a number like $100,000. A different time frame would have a much different meaning. For example, revenue of $100,000 a month is much different than revenue of $100,000 a year.

We can contrast temporary accounts, like revenue and expense accounts, with permanent accounts like cash. Saying we have $100,000 cash does not require a time frame to define what we mean because cash is a permanent account, representing a position at a point in time.

Expense - is the using of assets or incurrence of liabilities as part of operations to generate revenue. Expenses are what a business needs to consume to achieve the goal of revenue generation. Expenses are also temporary accounts needing a beginning and ending time.

There are usually many more expense accounts then revenue accounts, but we hope the revenue accounts add up to a greater dollar amount. The reason there are more expense accounts then revenue accounts is because of specialization, companies focusing on earning money by doing what they do best and paying for their other needs.

Expense accounts will vary from company to company but common expense accounts include utility expense, wages expense, auto expense, supplies expense, and meals and entertainment expense.

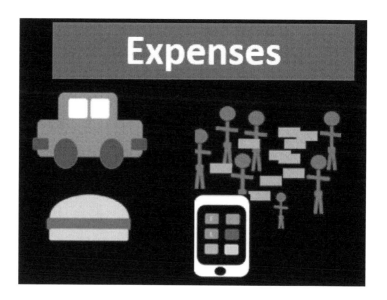

Ch. 6 The One Rule for Increasing and Decreasing Account Balances

Once we understand the normal balance of an account,

represented by the image below, there is only one rule we need to

know to make an account go up or down.

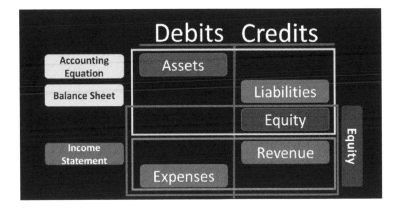

The one rule to make an account balance go up or down is: **do
the same to go up and opposite to go down.**

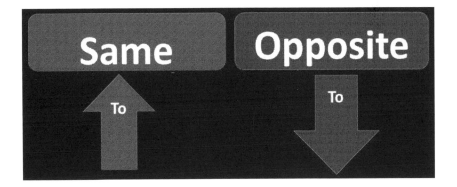

The one rule of, do the same to go up and opposite to go down,

may seem abstract at first but once we have the normal balance cheat

sheet above, it is easy to apply. The one rule means that an account with a normal debit balance will be increased by another debit because a debit is the same thing as the normal account balance, and an account with a normal credit balance will be increased by a credit because a credit is the same thing as the normal account balance. Conversely, an account with a normal debit balance will be decreased by a credit because a credit is the opposite of the normal account balance, and an account with a normal credit balance will be decreased by a debit because a debit is the opposite thing as the normal account balance.

Like most things, the one rule is best learned through doing. We will first look at how the one rule applies to individual accounts within account types, analyzing part of a transaction, and then move to analyzing full business transactions, full transactions involving at least two accounts.

Ch. 7 The One Rule Applied to Cash and Asset Accounts

As we move forward remember to keep the normal balances in mind and the one rule in mind because these are concepts we will continually return to. We will now consider the one rule as it applies to assets, accounts that have a normal debit balance, as can be seen on the cheat sheet below. The most common asset and the first account we want to consider for any transaction is cash. As we analyze how to apply the one rule to the cash account keep in mind that all asset accounts will be affected in much the same way, with the exception of contra asset account, a topic for another time.

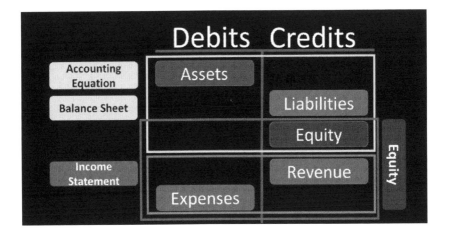

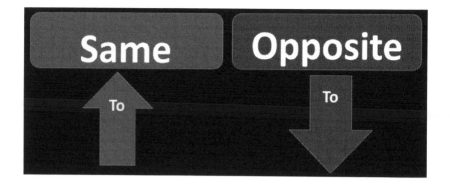

To consider the one rules effect on cash we will first assume our company received cash. Cash is an asset, assets having a normal debit balance according to our cheat sheet, and when we receive more cash, cash goes up, which leads to the question; how do we make the asset account of cash go up? Should we debit the cash account or credit the cash account to increase the account? From our normal balance cheat sheet, we see that cash has a normal debit balance. Applying our one rule to making accounts go up or down of, do the same to go up and opposite to go down, we would debit the cash account to make it go up. The cash account is an asset with a debit balance so the same thing as a debit is another debit, debits increasing the cash account.

Below is an example of cash going up using our board, our T-account, or ledger. Cash starts out with a normal debit balance of $1,000 and will be increased by $200 representing the company receiving cash. Note that this is only part of a financial transaction, this example not explaining why the company is receiving cash. We will cover many transactions shortly but we first need an understanding of accounts, normal balances, and how to make normal debit and credit accounts go up or down, these being the rules, the recording of transactions being the game.

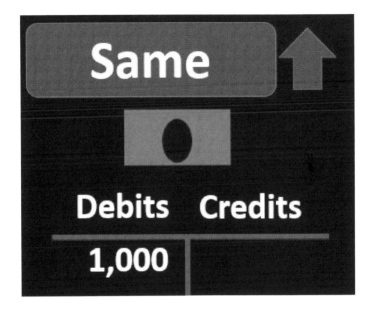

When the business received $200 we increase cash by adding the $200 to the left side, the debit side of the cash T-account, the cash board, or ledger, the result being an increase in the debit balance from $1,000 to $1,200. Our one rule states that we do the same to make an account balance go up and the opposite to make our account balance go down.

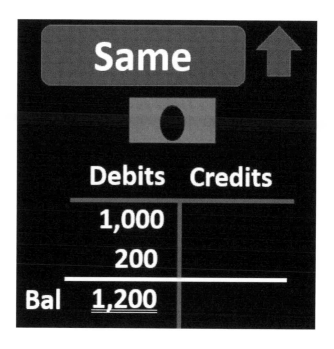

Examples allow us to analyze why the one rule works, why debiting a debit balance account and crediting a credit balance account makes the account go up and why crediting a debit balance account and debiting a credit balance account makes the account go down.

The T-account or ledger can be thought of as a kind of race track, pitting debits against credits, both sides trying to win, the winner claiming the normal balance of the account as either debit or credit. This game, however, is rigged or not fair, because we already know whom the winner will be by memorizing the normal balances. A cash account has a normal balance of a debit and therefore the debit side will always win the game, win the race. The only real question about the debit and credit race on the cash track, The T-account, or ledger, is; how much will debits win by? If we debit the cash account it may result in a huge debit victory, as the debits win by a wide margin over the credits. When we credit the cash account the result is a slowing down of the debit balance lead, a decrease in the amount the debits are winning by, a decrease in the account balance.

Note that the T-account or ledger is not in balance, meaning the debits do not equal the credits. The debits and credit are not in balance because we are only considering half the transaction, only looking a one account in a transaction, and all transactions must have at least two accounts. The entire transaction will be in balance and total debits and credits for all accounts will be equal when we record debits and credits for all accounts involved in the transaction. We will record complete transactions in a later section.

Now consider what happens when a company spends cash. Cash going out of the checking account leaves the accountant or bookkeeper asking the questions; how do we make the cash account go down? Do we debit or credit cash to make the cash account go down? Because cash is an asset account it has a debit balance according to our normal balance cheat sheet. Per our one rule, do the same to increase and the opposite to decrease, we must credit cash in order to make the account go down. Cash has a normal debit balance, and the opposite of a debit is a credit. Therefore, we must credit the cash account to make it go down.

Below is an example of cash going down using our board, or T-account, or ledger. Cash starts out with a normal balance of $1,000 and will be decreased by $200 representing the company paying cash. Note that this is only part of a financial transaction, this example not explaining why the company is paying cash. We will cover many transactions shortly but we first need an understanding of accounts, normal balances, and how to make normal debit and credit accounts go up or down, these being the rules, the recording of transactions being the game.

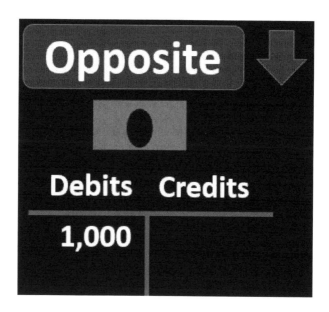

When the business pays $200 we decrease cash by adding the $200 to the right side, the credit side of the cash T-account, the cash board, or ledger, the result being an increase in the credits and a net decrease in the debit balance.

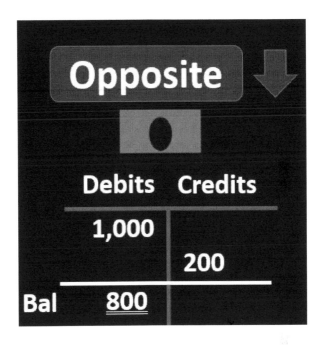

When the cash account is credited our one rule tells us that the balance will go down, credits being the opposite of the normal debit balance in the cash account but we can think about how the debit balance goes down a few different ways. When considering our race track analogy, we see that debits started out with a $1,000 lead. Then the credits start catching up by increasing the credit balance by $200, the result, total debit balance adding up to $1,000, the total credit balance adding up to $200, and the difference calculating out at $800 ($1,000 − $200).

It is also possible to consider a running balance, as a useful tool to analyze transactions, a running balance calculating the balance after each new transaction, debits increasing the cash running balance and credits decreasing the cash running balance. We will consider these methods further when discussing the general ledger in more detail.

According to our normal balance cheat sheet, asset accounts and expense accounts have normal debit balances and therefore, debits will make them go up and credits will make them go down. Note that any good rule has exceptions and there are contra accounts, accounts that have a normal balance that is the opposite of the normal balance in the account category. For example, accumulated depreciation is an asset that has a normal balance opposite to most assets, a credit normal balance. As always, rules must first be learned before learning when we must brake rules.

Asset accounts include: Cash, building, land, equipment, account receivable and supplies.

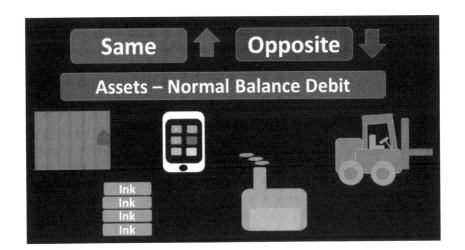

Ch. 8 The One Rule Applied to Accounts Payable and Liability Accounts

As we move forward remember to keep the normal balances in mind and the one rule in mind because these are concepts we will continually return to. We will now consider the one rule as it applies to liability accounts, accounts that have a normal credit balance as can be seen on the cheat sheet. The most common liability, and the first account we want to consider when thinking of liabilities, is accounts payable. As we analyze how to apply the one rule to the accounts payable account keep in mind that all liability accounts will be affected in much the same way.

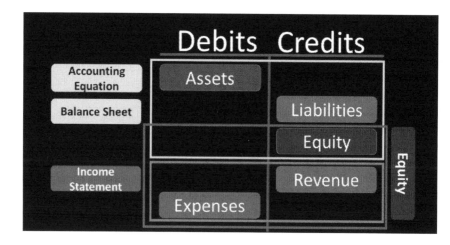

To consider the one rules effect on accounts payable we will first assume our company purchases something on account, the liability account of accounts payable going up, representing the company owing money in the future. Accounts payable is a liability account, liabilities having a normal credit balance according to our cheat sheet, and when we make a purchase on account, accounts payable goes up, which leads to the question; how do we make the liability account of accounts payable go up? Should we debit the accounts payable account or credit the accounts payable account to increase it? From our normal balance cheat sheet, we see that accounts payable has a normal credit balance. Applying our one rule to making accounts go up or down of, do the same to go up and opposite to go down, we would credit the accounts payable account to make it go up. The accounts payable account is a liability account with a normal credit balance and the same thing as a credit is another credit, credits increasing the liability account.

Below is an example of accounts payable going up using or board, or T-account, or ledger. Accounts payable starts out with a normal credit balance of $1,000 and will be increased by $200 representing the company purchasing something on account, that something not being defined because we do not want to distract from what is going on with accounts payable. We will cover the full transaction in a later section but we first need an understanding of accounts, normal balances, and how to make normal debit and credit accounts go up or down, these being the rules, the recording of transactions being the game.

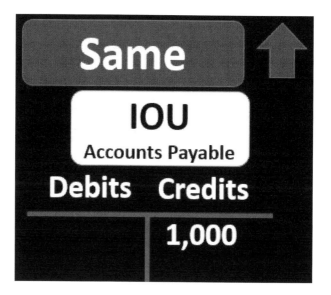

When the business purchases something worth $200 on account we increase accounts payable by adding the $200 to the right side, the credit side of the accounts payable T-account, the accounts payable board, or ledger, the result, an increase in the credit balance from $1,000 to $1,200. Our one rule states that we do the same to make an account balance go up and the opposite to make our account balance go down.

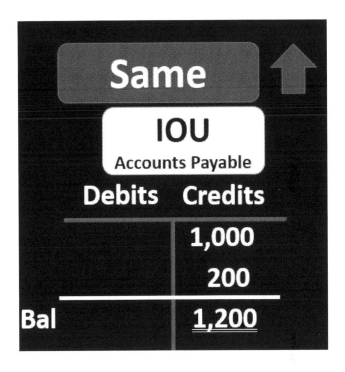

The same race track analogy we used to analyze the normal debit balance of cash can be used to describe the normal credit balance of accounts payable and liabilities, the debits and credits racing against each other, both trying to gain more on their side of the track, to claim the prize of being the normal balance of the account. The game, however, is rigged or determined, the credits always resulting as the winners when considering liability accounts, like accounts payable. A credit will increase the amount by which credits will win, increasing the normal balance of the account in the credit direction. A debit will decrease the amount by which credits will win, decreasing the normal balance of the account. The debits can never win, never be greater than the credits in a liability account, but they can work to reduce the difference, to bring down the margin.

Now consider what happens when a company pays off the accounts payable balance, reducing what is owed for a purchase made in the past. The amount owed goes down which leaves the accountant or bookkeeper asking the questions; how do we make the amount owed go down; how to we make the accounts payable account go down? Do we debit accounts payable to make it go down or credit accounts payable to make it go down? Because accounts payable is a liability account it has a credit balance according to our normal balance cheat sheet. Per our one rule of, do the same to increase and the opposite to decrease, we must debit accounts payable in order to make the account go down. Accounts payable has a normal credit balance and the opposite of a credit is a debit. Therefore, we must debit the accounts payable account to make it go down.

Below is an example of accounts payable going down using our board, or T-account, or ledger. Cash starts out with a normal credit balance of $1,000 and will be decreased by $200 representing the company paying off the balance due. Note that this is only part of a financial transaction, this example not focusing on the decrease in cash because we are considering the accounts payable account. We will cover the full transaction in a later section.

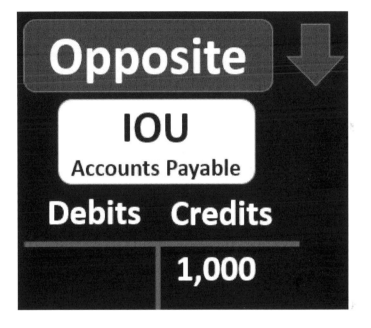

When the business reduces the accounts payable account by paying off the $200 balance due we decrease accounts payable by adding the $200 to the left side, the debit side, of the accounts payable T-account, the accounts payable board or ledger. The result is an increase in the debits and a net decrease in the total credit balance.

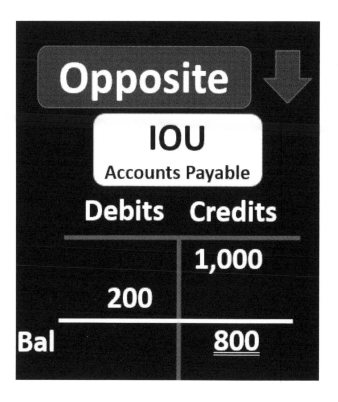

When the accounts payable account is debited our one rule tells us that the balance will go down, debits being the opposite of the normal credit balance in the accounts payable account but we can think about how the credit balance goes down a few different ways. When considering our race track analogy, we see that credits started out with a $1,000 lead and the debits starting to catch up by increasing the debit balance by $200. The result is the total credit balance adding up to $1,000, the total debit balance adding up to $200, and the difference calculating out at a credit of $800 ($1,000 – $200).

All liability accounts will act in a similar way as accounts payable, all liability accounts having a normal credit balance, resulting in credits increasing liability accounts, and debits decreasing liability accounts.

Liability accounts include: accounts payable, notes payable, salaries payable, and unearned revenue.

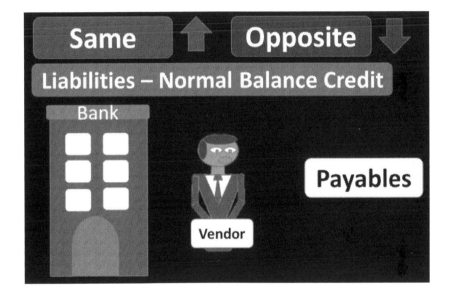

Ch. 9 The One Rule Applied to Equity Accounts

We will now consider the one rule as it applies to equity accounts, accounts that have a normal credit balance as can be seen on the cheat sheet. The equity section can be confusing, equity on the balance sheet representing equity as a whole as, of a point in time, but temporary accounts, including income and expense accounts, are part of the story of the equity section reported on the balance sheet. Here we will focus on the capital account, the account reporting net assets on the balance sheet for a sole proprietorship. Note that a partnership will have much the same reporting but will have more than one capital account because a partnership has more than one owner, and a corporation will include stockholder's equity, stockholder's being the owners of a corporation. No matter the structure of the organization the equity section, taken a whole, will act in much the same way.

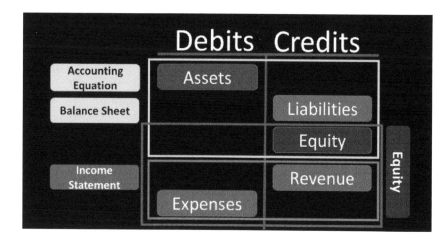

To consider the one rule's effect on capital we will first think about the impact on the capital account when our owner invests money into the business. Capital is an equity account, most equity accounts having a normal credit balance according to our cheat sheet, and when an owner invests into a company, the capital account goes up, which leads to the question; how do we make the equity account of capital go up? Should we debit the capital account or credit the capital account to increase it? From our normal balance cheat sheet, we see that capital has a normal credit balance. Applying our one rule to making accounts go up or down of, do the same to go up and opposite to go down, we would credit the capital account to make it go up. The capital account is an equity account with a normal credit balance and the same thing as a credit is another credit, credits increasing the capital account.

Below is an example of the capital account going up using our board, or T-account, or ledger. Capital starts out with a normal credit balance of $1,000 and will be increased by $200 representing the owner investing money into the company. Note that we are only concentrating on one side of the transaction, focusing in on what happens to the capital account. We will cover the full transaction in a later section but we first need an understanding of accounts, normal balances, and how to make normal debit and credit accounts go up or down, these being the rules, the recording of transactions being the game.

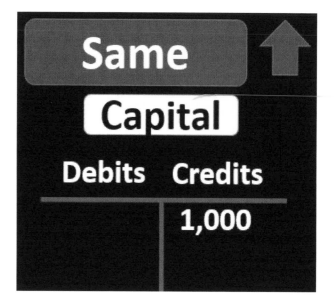

When an owner invests $200 into the business we increase the capital account by adding the $200 to the right side, the credit side of the capital T-account, the capital account board or ledger, the result, an increase in the credit balance from $1,000 to $1,200. Our one rule states that we do the same to make an account balance go up and the opposite to make our account balance go down.

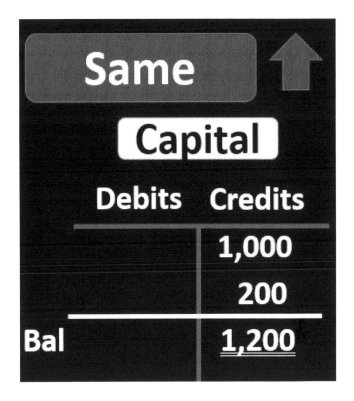

Although capital generally has a credit balance there is an exception to this normal balance rule. If the assets are less than the liabilities the capital account would result in a net debit balance, indicating that the business has negative net assets.

The capital account will go down with a debit, a debit being the opposite of the normal balance of the capital account. The capital account does not often receive a debit directly, however, but will receive debit transactions when closing out temporary accounts, when closing out the income statement accounts and draws. We will discuss the closing process in another text but for now, we will think of the capital account as a whole, as an amount that includs income and expense accounts. We will then analyze the income statement accounts of revenue and expense separately from the capital account.

Revenue is a credit component of the capital balance and will have a similar effect on the capital account as the owner investment, the capital account increasing when revenue increases. It is useful to know that temporary accounts, like revenue accounts, usually only go up, revenue never generally going down. Net income, revenue minus expenses, will go down, but revenue generally only goes up, and it goes up with credits. Remember that temporary accounts are accounts dealing with timing, with measuring performance. Income statement accounts of revenue and expense are temporary accounts, needing a beginning and ending time to make sense. Balance sheet accounts are not temporary accounts but permanent accounts, only requiring one date when being represented.

Now consider what happens when an owner withdraws money from the business, reducing what is owed to the owner, reducing the net value of the business. A draw would result in the net capital account going down. Note that draws will often be recorded in a separate, temporary account, which will then be closed to the capital account, but we will consider the net effect on the capital account now. Once we determine that capital needs to go down we are left with the questions; how do we make the capital account go down? Do we debit the capital account to make it go down or credit the capital account to make it go down? Because the capital account is an equity account it has a normal credit balance according to our normal balance cheat sheet. Per our one rule of, do the same to increase and the opposite to decrease, we must debit the capital account to make the account go down. The capital account has a normal credit balance and the opposite of a credit is a debit. Therefore, we must debit the capital account to make it go down.

Below is an example of the capital account going down using our board, our T-account, or ledger. Capital starts out with a normal credit balance of $1,000 and will be decreased by $200 representing the owner withdrawing cash. Note that this is only part of a financial transaction, this example not focusing on the decrease in cash because we are focusing on the capital account. We will cover the full transaction in a later section.

When the business reduces the capital account due to the owner drawing $200 out of the business we decrease the capital account by adding the $200 to the left side, the debit side, of the capital T-account, the capital account board or ledger. The result is an increase in the debits and a net decrease in the total credit balance.

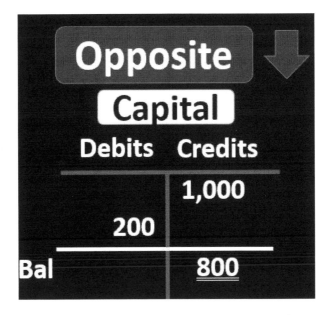

All expense accounts are debit components of the capital account and will have a similar effect on the capital account as the owner draws, the capital account decreasing when expenses increase. It is useful to know that temporary accounts, like expense accounts, usually only go up, expenses never generally going down. Net income, revenue minus expenses, will go down, but expenses generally only go up. The debit balance of expense accounts is the opposite of the capital account's normal credit balance and will therefore decrease total capital.

Equity accounts include: Owner's capital for a sole proprietor, multiple owner's capital accounts for a partnership, and retained earnings and stockholder's equity for a corporation. For all entity types, total equity includes the temporary income statement accounts of revenue and expense accounts. Total equity also includes temporary accounts that represent the distribution of resources to owners, including draws for a sole proprietorship and partnership and dividends for a corporation.

Ch. 10 The One Rule Applied to Revenue Accounts

We will now consider the one rule as it applies to revenue accounts, accounts that have a normal credit balance as can be seen on the cheat sheet. Most businesses have one or two primary revenue accounts because they specialize in one or two things to generate revenue. The revenue account may be called sales, income, or simply revenue, depending on the industry and preference of the business. As we analyze how to apply the one rule to the revenue account keep in mind that all revenue accounts will be effected in much the same way.

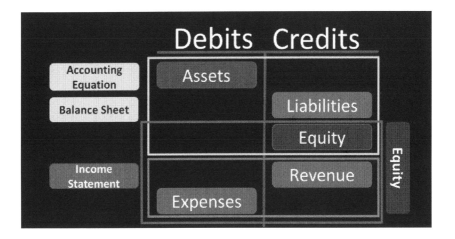

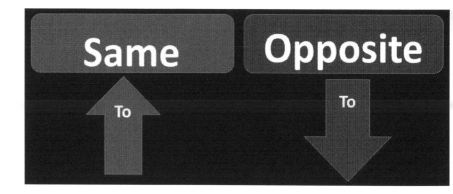

To analyze the effect of our one rule for increasing and decreasing revenue accounts, we will first consider how revenue increases because of a sale made by a service business. We will start off thinking about a service business to eliminate the added element of tracking inventory and will add this element in a later text.

When a company makes a sale a question to record the transaction is: should we debit the revenue account or credit revenue to increase it? From our normal balance cheat sheet, we see that revenue has a normal credit balance. Applying our one rule to making revenue go up or down of, do the same to go up and opposite to go down, we would credit the revenue account to make it go up. The revenue account has a normal credit balance and the same thing as a credit is another credit, credits increasing the revenue account.

Below is an example of revenue going up using our board, or, T-account or ledger. Revenue starts out with a normal credit balance of

$1,000 and will be increased by $200 representing the company making a sale. Note that we are only considering the sales side of the transaction and not the payment side, the cash received, or increase in accounts receivable, because we are focusing in on how the revenue account works. We will cover the full transaction in a later section but we first need an understanding of accounts, normal balances, and how to make normal debit and credit accounts go up or down, these being the rules, the recording of transactions being the game.

When a sale is made for $200 we increase the revenue account by adding the $200 to the right side, the credit side, of the revenue T-account, the revenue account board or ledger, the result being an increase in the credit balance from $1,000 to $1,200. Our one rule states that we do the same to make an account balance go up and the opposite to make our account balance go down.

The revenue account is a temporary account, an account that needs a beginning and ending date to make sense, and temporary accounts generally only go one way. The revenue account generally only goes up and it does so with credits. The revenue account tracks how many credits have accumulated on the right side of the T-account, and therefore how much income we have earned over time.

When determining whether an account is temporary or permanent, we can ask the question: do we need a time frame, a beginning and ending date, to make the account balance make sense. For example, if somebody says they earn $100,000, do we need a time frame for this statement to make sense. When we see a number like $100,000 we often automatically apply the time frame of one year, but a time frame is needed for the statement to make sense, a time frame like $100,000 a month, $100,000 a year, or $100,000 a lifetime. The balance sheet account of cash does not need such a time frame. For example, if somebody says they have $100,000 cash, we do not need a beginning and ending date for this statement to make sense because the cash balance is as of a point in time.

It is also useful to remember that balance sheet accounts are permanent accounts and income statement accounts are temporary, permanent accounts having a normal balance but often going both up and down, experiencing both debits and credits. Temporary accounts also have a normal balance but often only going up in one direction, experiencing only debits or credits, but not both.

Below is an example of how revenue would go down with a debit, debits being opposite to the normal balance, but it is crossed out to help us remember that revenue generally only goes up, generally experiencing only credits and not debits.

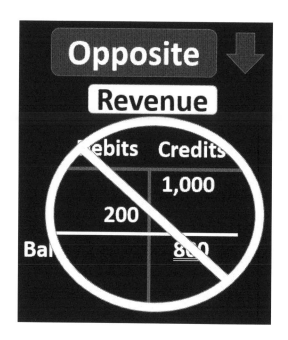

Companies usually only have one or two revenue accounts because businesses will specialize in the revenue generation activities. The revenue account may be called sales for merchandising companies, fees earned for service companies, or have a generic name like revenue or income. No matter the name, revenue accounts will act in a similar way, always increasing with credits, until they are closed out. We will talk about the closing process in a later text.

Ch. 11 The One Rule Applied to Expense Accounts

We will now consider the one rule as it applies to expense accounts, accounts that have a normal debit balance as can be seen on the cheat sheet. Most businesses will have many expense accounts because they will specialize in a specific money generating activity and pay for the rest of their needs, the rest of their needs resulting in expenses. Expense accounts will vary depending on the industry and preference of the business, but many will be common to most businesses like salaries expense, utility expense, and depreciation expense. As we analyze the how to apply the one rule to the expense accounts keep in mind that all expense accounts behave in much the same way.

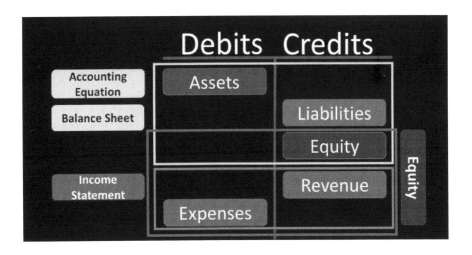

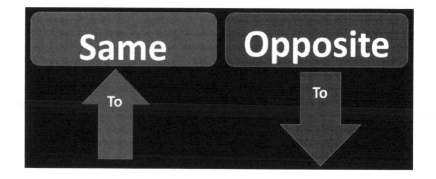

To analyze the effect of our one rule for increasing and decreasing expense accounts we will first consider the telephone expense account increasing because of a payment made for the phone service.

When a company pays the telephone bill a question to record the transaction is: should we debit the telephone expense account or credit the telephone expense account to increase it? From our normal balance cheat sheet, we see that expenses have a normal debit balance. Applying our one rule to making accounts go up or down of, do the same to go up and opposite to go down, we would debit the telephone expense account to make it go up. The telephone expense account has a normal debit balance and the same thing as a debit is another debit, debits increasing the telephone expense account.

Below is an example of the telephone expense account going up using our board, or T-account, or ledger. Telephone expense starts out with a normal debit balance of $1,000 and will be increased by $200 representing the company paying the telephone bill. Note that we are only considering the expense side of the transaction and not the payment side, the cash paid, because we are focusing on how the expense accounts work. We will cover the full transaction in a later section but we first need an understanding of accounts, normal balances, and how to make normal debit and credit accounts go up or down, these being the rules, the recording of transactions being the game.

When the telephone bill is paid for $200 we increase the expense account by adding the $200 to the left side, the debit side of the expense T-account, the expense account board or ledger. The result is an increase in the debit balance from $1,000 to $1,200. Our one rule states that we do the same to make an account balance go up and the opposite to make our account balance go down.

The expense accounts are temporary accounts, accounts that need a beginning and ending date to make sense, and temporary accounts generally only go one way. Expense accounts generally only go up and they do so with debits, the expense accounts tracking how many debits, and therefore how much expense, we have incurred over time.

When determining whether an account is temporary or permanent we can ask the question: do we need a time frame, a beginning and ending date, to make the account balance make sense. For example, if somebody says their rent expense is $1,000, do we need a time frame for this statement to make since? When we see a number like $1,000 related to rent expense we often automatically apply the time frame of one month, but a time frame is needed for the statement to make sense, a time frame like $1,000 a week, $1,000 a month, or $1,000 a year. In contrast to income statement accounts, the balance sheet account of cash does not need such a time frame. For example, if somebody says they have $1,000 cash, we do not need a beginning and ending date for this statement to make sense because the cash balance is as of a point in time.

It is also useful to remember that balance sheet accounts are permanent accounts and income statement accounts are temporary, permanent accounts having a normal balance but often going both up and down, experiencing both debits and credits. Temporary accounts also have a normal balance but often only go up in one direction, experiencing only debits or credits, but not both.

Below is an example of how an expense account would go down with a credit, credits being opposite to the normal balance, but it is crossed out to help us remember that expense accounts generally only go up, generally experiencing only debits and not credits.

Companies will have many expense accounts including utility expense, salaries expense, depreciation expense, telephone expense, supplies expense, and meals and entertainment expense. Merchandising companies will also include cost of goods sold representing the expense of inventory sold. All expense accounts will act in much the same way, constantly increasing with debits, until they are closed out. We will talk about the closing process in another text.

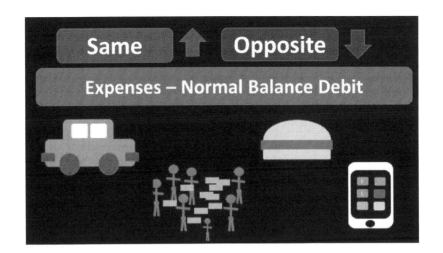

Ch. 12 Transaction Rules Using Debits and Credits

Now that we have an idea of how to make individual accounts go up or down using our one rule, we can apply this knowledge to making transactions. Don't worry if we do not yet fully understand how to make each account go up and down because this understanding is best achieved through generating transactions, as we will do soon. Recording full transactions will allow us to use techniques to determine how to record less familiar accounts. When we record full transactions, we can start building the journal entries by focusing on what we know, making it easier to figure out the portions of transactions we do not know. As we work through transactions we will refine the technique of focusing first on what we know and using this knowledge to complete the full transaction. We will start with transaction rules, then learn some terminology about what a general ledger and trial balance are, then consider our transaction thought process, and then use this knowledge to record and post full transactions; finally.

In our last book, Accounting Instruction Reference #100, we provided the following rules when analyzing transactions using the accounting equation:

- Every transaction will affect at least two accounts.
- Every transaction will keep the accounting equation in balance.

The first rule still applies when recording transactions using debits and credits. The balancing concept of the second rule will still apply but will be represented it in a different way. Transaction rules for recording transactions using debits and credits are:

- Every transaction will affect at least two accounts.
- Every transaction will have an equal amount reported for debits and credits

After learning the balancing concepts related to the accounting equation using simple math, math we all know love, many people question the need for learning debits in credits. In other words, why do we need debits and credits when we can express the balancing concept using the accounting equation?

Although the accounting equation does a great job of representing the balancing concept, it does not hold up well when compiling data to construct the financial statements because we cannot easily use the accounting equation to represent the data in a condensed form, like a trial balance. The accounting equation also results in some transactions that have no effect on the accounting equation, which can be confusing. For example, purchasing equipment for cash would result in one asset going up and another asset going down, the net result being no effect on the accounting

equation. The format of the accounting equation also makes the

breaking out of income statement accounts, revenue and expense

accounts, more difficult, these accounts being grouped in the equity

section if the accounting equation.

Because of the limits on the use of the accounting equation

debits and credit are the primary building material used to record

the financial transactions and construct financial statements.

Debits	Credits
1,000	
	200
	800
Bal 1,000	1,000

After learning how to apply debits and credits to individual

accounts and how to make, and demonstrate, individual accounts go up

or down using a T-account, it may seem unusual that our second rule

states that total debits and credits must always be equal for each

transaction. The T-accounts we have worked with for individual accounts have not had an even number of debits and credits. Although individual accounts will not have an equal number of debits and credits, each transaction will have at least two accounts impacted, and total debits and credits will be equal for the total transaction. Each individual account, however, will have a normal balance of debit or credit, debits or credits winning the race for each individual account.

Total debits and credits, taken as a whole, will also be the same, total debits for all accounts equaling total credits for all accounts. We will demonstrate this using a trial balance in the next section but for now, we can analyze our normal balance cheat sheet and note that if we were to add up the balance in all account categories, total debits would equal total credits. In other words, debit accounts of assets and expenses would equal credit accounts of liabilities, equity, and revenue.

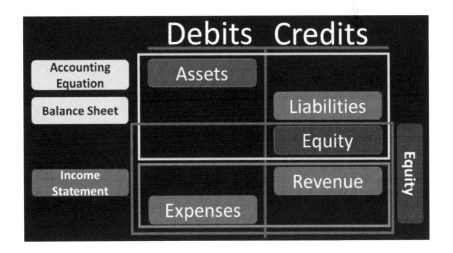

Ch. 13 General Ledger & Trial Balance

Now that we know transaction rules, we need to consider some terminology related to recording transactions, the terms general ledger and trial balance.

The general ledger will look familiar because our T-account is a shorthand way to represent the general ledger, the general ledger recording the detail of transactions in each account, ordering transaction detail by date. For example, our cash T-account example started with a beginning balance of $1,000 and was decreased by a $200 transaction to arrive at a balance of $800. The general ledger allows us to see the detail behind the account balance of $800, to see the $1,000 beginning balance, and $200 transaction.

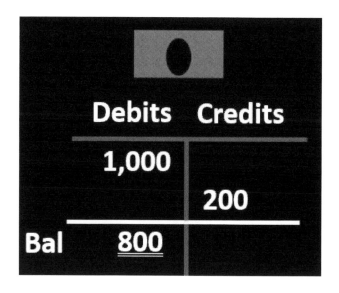

A T-account works great for short calculations but where more transactions are needed it is helpful to see dates and a running balance. Below is an example of a general ledger showing more transactions which include dates of transactions and a running balance of the account total for each date.

Cash-Checking			
Date	Debit	Credit	Balance
Beginning Balance			0
1/1	3,000		3,000
1/3	8,000		11,000
1/5		(5,000)	6,000
1/5		(80)	5,920
1/8	360		6,280
1/12		(75)	6,205
1/16		(1,000)	5,205
1/16	250		5,455
1/18		(175)	5,280
1/19		(40)	5,240
1/23	720		5,960
1/24	200		6,160
1/26	150		6,310
1/26		(75)	6,235
1/28	425		6,660
1/31		(500)	6,160
Bal	13,105	(6,945)	6,160

Note that we can still make out the T-account, the debits on the left and the credits on the right. Total debits of $13,105 minus total credits of $6,945 results in a debit balance in the cash account of $6,160. Added to the standard T-account, the general ledger includes dates, emphasizing that the general ledger is ordered by the date of the transaction, and subtotals, allowing us to see the account balance at any transaction date.

Take some time to analyze how the running balance is calculated, taking the prior balance, adding debits and subtracting credits, debits increasing this account because cash is an asset account with a normal debit balance. For example, the beginning balance is $0; the first transaction is a debit of $3,000, resulting in a running balance of $3,000. The second transaction is a debit of $8,000, resulting in a running balance of $11,000 ($8,000 + $3,000). The next transaction is a credit of $5,000, resulting in a running balance of $6,000 ($11,000 - $5,000).

Note that credits are being represented with brackets (). Different software will represent credits in a variety of ways but using brackets can be useful because it allows us to represent debits and credits in one column and can help simplify calculations like net income. For example, the total balance column in the image above does not show a debit and credit column, but just one column. Part of the reason only one column is needed is that most accounts have a set normal balance of either debit or credit, eliminating the need for two columns in the running balance section, but we will encounter accounts in future texts that can flip from a debit balance to a credit balance. Representing credits with brackets () can simplify our worksheets in these cases.

Each account will have its own general ledger account just as each account had its own T-account, each account having a normal balance of either debit or credit. Accounts with a normal credit balance will increase with a credit and decrease with a debt, just as they had with our T-account example of the accounts payable account. Below is an example of accounts payable general ledger.

Accounts Payable			
Date	Debit	Credit	Balance
Beginning Balance			0
1/1		(1,500)	(1,500)
1/5		(185)	(1,685)
1/8		(315)	(2,000)
1/10		(140)	(2,140)
1/15	175		(1,965)
1/18	75		(1,890)
Bal	250	(2,140)	(1,890)

The account starts out with a 0 balance and is increased with a credit of $1,500, bringing the balance to $1,500. The account is then increased with a credit of $185, bringing the balance to $1,685 (1,500 + 185). On 1/10 the balance is $2,140 and on 1/15 the account is debited for $175, bringing the running balance down to $1,965 ($2,140 – $175).

We will not go through each general ledger account in this section but we will revisit them when recording transactions.

A trial balance will list all accounts that have a balance and show the account balance as of a specific date, the account balance being drawn from the general ledger, the trial balance being constructed from the general ledger. Below is an example of the trial balance. Note that we can still see our T format, but now the T represents debit and credit account balances for all accounts and is similar to our normal balance cheat sheet. The green accounts are assets with normal debit balances, the orange accounts are liabilities with normal credit balances, and the equity accounts are light blue and usually have normal credit balance. The income statement accounts are dark blue, including revenue, with a normal credit balance, and expenses, with a normal debit balance.

Accounts	Debits	Credits
Cash-Checking	6,160	
Accounts Receivable	800	
Landscaping Supplies	325	
Prepaid insurance	1,000	
Auto	5,000	
Acc. Depr. - Auto	0	
Lawn Equipment	1,500	
Acc. Depr. - Lawn Equipment	0	
Accounts Payable		(1,890)
Notes payable		(8,000)
Interest Payable		0
Unearned Revenue		(360)
Capital		(3,000)
Drawing	500	
Revenue		(2,545)
Landscaping Supplies Expense	0	
Auto Expense	120	
Advertising Expense	315	
Equipment Rental Expense	75	
Insurance Expense	0	
Depreciation Expense - Auto	0	
Depreciation Expense - Lawn I	0	
Interest Expense	0	
Total Debits - Total (credits)	15,795	(15,795)
Net Income		(2,035)

As we can see our trial balance has a total debit column of $15,795 and a total credit column of $15,795, total debits matching total credits. Net income can be calculated as revenue minus expenses, or income statement credit balance accounts less income statement debit balance accounts, resulting in net income of $2,035. Note that credits are being reported with brackets (), computer software recognizing credits as negative numbers in this case. Representing credits with ()s, or negative numbers, is useful because it allows us to show that total debits equal total credits through subtraction, total debits equaling total credits resulting in total debits minus total credits being zero.

Below is a trial balance with just one column, debits represented without brackets, credits represented with brackets. Note how this format allows us to use only one column and perform some simple calculations in software like Excel. For example, net income can be calculated by simply summing the dark blue income statement accounts of revenue and expenses, Excel subtracting debits and credits. Total equity can be calculated as assets minus liabilities by summing up all asset and liability accounts, Excel subtracting the liability credit balances from asset debit balances.

Accounts	Trial Balance
Cash-Checking	6,160
Accounts Receivable	800
Landscaping Supplies	325
Prepaid insurance	1,000
Auto	5,000
Acc. Depr. - Auto	0
Lawn Equipment	1,500
Acc. Depr. - Lawn Equipment	0
Accounts Payable	(1,890)
Notes payable	(8,000)
Interest Payable	0
Unearned Revenue	(360)
Capital	(3,000)
Drawing	500
Revenue	(2,545)
Landscaping Supplies Expense	0
Auto Expense	120
Advertising Expense	315
Equipment Rental Expense	75
Insurance Expense	0
Depreciation Expense - Auto	0
Depreciation Expense - Lawn E	0
Interest Expense	0
Total Debits - Total (credits)	0
Net Income	(2,035)

One of the most challenging aspects of learning debits and credits is to distinguish the concept of debits and credits from the adding and subtracting of debits and credits. This problem of differentiating debits and credits from adding and subtracting, even while we are using the operation of addition and subtraction when working with debits and credits, is a problem every student must struggle with. The best way to fully understand the difference is by performing transactions, transactions we will start performing soon.

Ch. 14 Transaction Thought Process

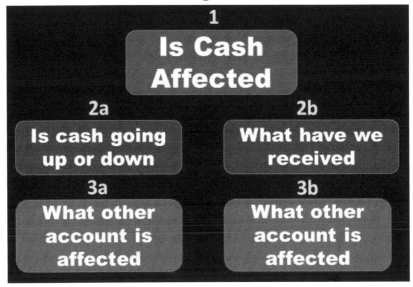

Now that we have the tools we need to record transactions we will discuss a thought process that we will use when recording every transaction. This thought process will make figuring out how to construct journal entries simpler by first directing us to build the part of the journal entry we know. Once we have created the part of the journal entry we know, it will help us figure out the rest of the journal entry.

The account we will become most familiar with when recording transactions is an account we already know well. Cash will be affected in about 75% of all transactions and is involved in most business cycles at some point. A great attribute of cash being involved in a transaction is the ease with which cash can be determined to be going up or down.

Cash goes up when money is received, and down when paid. Once we know the direction of the cash account this knowledge will help with recording the rest of the journal entry. For the reasons above our first question when recording any transaction is: is cash affected?

Question 1 – Is cash affected in this transaction?

If the answer is yes, and it will be for most transactions, we will then consider whether cash is going up or down.

Question 2a – Is cash going up or down in this transaction?

Once we understand which way cash is going, up or down, cash coming or going, we can use our one rule to post the cash portion of the journal entry. Because cash is an asset with a debit balance a debit will increase the cash account and a credit will decrease the cash account. Therefore, if cash needs to go up, we will debit cash, and if cash needs to go down, we will credit cash. Once we have constructed the portion of the journal entry related to cash we can use this information to help build the rest of the journal entry, leading to our next question: what other account is affected?

Question 3a – What other account is affected in this transaction?

The non-cash account, or accounts, are often harder to determine and more difficult to understand than the cash account, the direction of the account and the need for a debit or credit, less clear. Once we know the direction of the cash account, we can use this understanding to help with the other accounts in the transactions. Most transactions, especially those we start out with, will only have two accounts affected.

For example, a transaction of paying the utility bill for $100 will result in cash going down with a credit, the cash portion of the transaction being obvious, the company decreasing cash. Once we record the credit to cash we know the second account must have a debit balance to keep the journal entry in balance, assuming only two accounts affected. All we need to know than, is what the second account name should be. When a business pays the utility bill an expense account called utility expense is used. Therefore, the transaction to record the payment of the utility bill would be a debit to utility expense and a credit to cash.

At this point recording transactions will still seem abstract, most learners not fully understanding until we actually post many journal entries, which we will do in the next section. The process of focusing on the cash portion of the transaction leads to the question of how we treat those other 25% of transactions where cash is not part of the journal entry. What is the thought process for these transactions where cash is not affected?

If we go back to question 1, is cash affected, and the answer is no, then we will focus on what we have received in the transaction.

Question 2b – What have we received in the transaction?

When no cash is affected in the transaction we will focus first on what we have received in the transaction because the posting of debits and credits is often more obvious for this portion of the transaction.

For example, if we purchased supplies on account, we will focus first on what we have received. The company has received supplies in this case. Supplies are an asset and assets have normal debit balances and therefore will go up with a debit. Once we know whether to debit or credit supplies we can use this understanding to help construct the rest of the journal entry.

Question 3b – What other account is affected?

After we have constructed half the transaction related to what the company has received, we can use this information to help build the rest of the journal entry.

For example, if we purchase supplies on account, and we first record the supplies asset account going up with a debit, we know the second account must be credited if there are only two accounts affected. All we need to know than, is what the second account name should be. When a business purchases on credit the liability account generally used is call account payable, and therefore, the transaction to record the purchase of supplies on account would be a debit to supplies and a credit to accounts payable.

The thought process below will become easier to understand and put into practical use after it has been put to practical use to help record many transactions, and recording transactions is what we will now do.

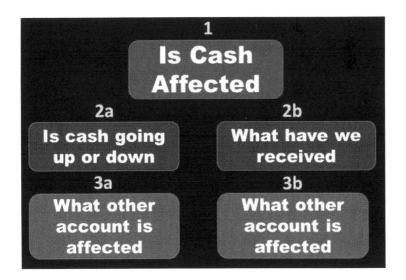

Ch. 15 Recording Transactions where Cash is Affected

      We will now start recording full transactions; finally. The transactions we will start with will be those that include cash as part of the transaction for a few reasons. Cash will be affected in most transactions and understanding cash will help us construct the rest of the transactions we create. Cash is the first account we think about when applying our thought process to recording transactions.

      As we record transactions keep our normal balance cheat sheet cheat sheet close by because it will be useful in constructing future journal entries.

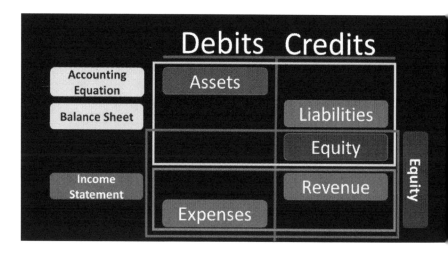

Transactions will be recorded in the general journal. The general journal is just the location were the journal entries are recorded. The act of creating the journal entry is called journalizing. Once the journal entry has been created it is posted to the general ledger. The general ledger is then used to generate the trial balance. In a computerized system, the posting process and the creation of the trial balance are automated. In order to see the big picture, to see what happens to the accounts a whole, we will start by posting transactions to a worksheet rather than a general ledger. At the end of this text, we will work a comprehensive problem that will post journal entries to a general ledger and use the general ledger to construct a trial balance.

The first transaction we will record is an owner depositing cash into a business of $100,000.

It is helpful to see the trial balance when recording transactions because the trial balance will list the accounts in order of assets, liabilities, equity, revenue, and expense. Our trial balance also color codes the account categories with green, orange, light blue, dark blue, and dark blue accordingly. Dark blue is used for all income statement accounts, income statement accounts including revenue and expense accounts.

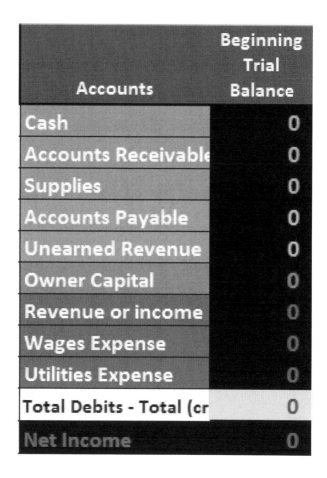

Accounts	Beginning Trial Balance
Cash	0
Accounts Receivable	0
Supplies	0
Accounts Payable	0
Unearned Revenue	0
Owner Capital	0
Revenue or income	0
Wages Expense	0
Utilities Expense	0
Total Debits - Total (cr	0
Net Income	0

When applying our thought process, we first ask whether cash is affected. The answer is yes because cash is going into the business from the owner, resulting in the businesses cash going up. Once we know what is happing to cash we will **wright this part of the journal entry**

down. Cash is an asset with a normal balance of a debit so we need to do the same thing to it to make cash go up which is another debit.

Accounts	Debit	(Credit)
Cash	100,000	

If only two accounts are effected we know the second account well must be credited for 100,000 so that the journal entry remains in balance, so we will **write this down**.

Accounts	Debit	(Credit)
Cash	100,000	
		(100,000)

Now we just need to figure out what the other account is which is affected. Looking at a trial balance helps us find the second account because the trial balance provides a list of accounts in order of assets, liabilities, equity, revenue, and expense. We know the **owner** put cash of $100,000 into the business, so it would be reasonable that we would be looking for an equity account, a light blue account, that account being the owner capital account. Because we figured out the cash half of the transaction we already know the capital account will be credited, so we will **write this down**.

Accounts	Debit	(Credit)
Cash	100,000	
Owner Capital		(100,000)

The journal entry is now complete, but we have not analyzed why we have credited the capital account, just entering a credit because we debited cash. Examining the second account will provide a double check that the transaction has been recorded correctly, and provide a better understanding of how the second account behaves. The capital account is an equity account. Equity accounts have a credit balance per our normal balance cheat sheet. The company owes the owner more money so the capital account should go up. Another way to understand why the capital account is going up is to realize that the net book value of the company is going up, asset minus liabilities going up, and therefore capital needs to go up, capital representing net assets. We make an account go up by doing the same thing as what its normal balance is, the capital account having a normal balance of a credit, resulting in a credit increasing the capital account.

Below is an illustration showing the beginning trial balance before our journal entry, a column representing our journal entry, and the trial balance after our journal entry has been recorded.

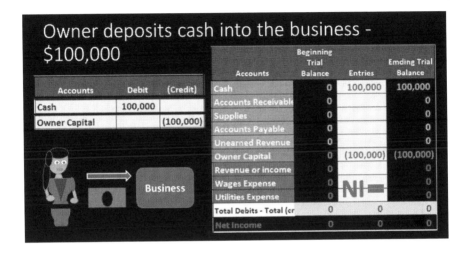

Note that the journal entry is representing debits and credits using a debit and credit column and using brackets () s for credits. The trial balance is representing debits and credit as unbracketed numbers for debits and bracketed numbers for credits, this format allowing us to represent the result of the transaction with three columns rather than using six columns. The green zeros represent that debits minus credits added up to zero in our beginning trial balance column, in our entries column, and therefore in our ending trial balance column. The green zeros show that the total debits equal the total credits in each column. Notice there is no effect on net income from this transaction even though cash went up, represented by the fact that there is no entry in any of the dark blue accounts, the income statement accounts, the

revenue and expense accounts.

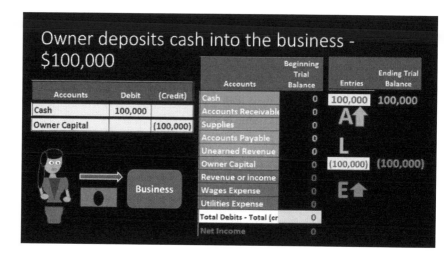

Analyzing the effect on the accounting equation we see that

assets are going up due to the asset of cash going up, liabilities are not

affected, and equity is going up due to the capital account going up.

Therefore, we see that the accounting equation also remains in balance,

assets going up on the left side and equity going up on the right side.

In the next transaction, the business receives cash for work completed of $10,000

Accounts	Beginning Trial Balance
Cash	100,000
Accounts Receivable	0
Supplies	0
Accounts Payable	0
Unearned Revenue	0
Owner Capital	(100,000)
Revenue or income	0
Wages Expense	0
Utilities Expense	0
Total Debits - Total (cr	0
Net Income	0

Starting off with our first question of the thought process; is cash affected, we see that cash is affected, the company receiving cash from a customer, so we will **write this part of the journal entry down**. Cash is an asset with a normal balance of a debit, so we need to do the same thing to it to make cash go up, which is another debit.

Accounts	Debit	(Credit)
Cash	10,000	

If there are only two accounts affected we know the second

account must be credited for $10,000, so we will **write this down**.

Accounts	Debit	(Credit)
Cash	10,000	
		(10,000)

Now, all we need to figure out is what the second account

affected is. If the company did work and has received cash at the same

time the company has earned revenue, revenue being the second

account affected, **so we will write this down**.

Accounts	Debit	(Credit)
Cash	10,000	
Revenue or income		(10,000)

Note that many beginners have a difficult time distinguishing

the concept of cash from the concept of revenue, cash and revenue

often happening at the same time, but they are not the same thing.

Cash is a form of payment while revenue represent the earning of value.

Revenue happens when work has been done while the payment could happen before, at the same time, or after the work has been done.

We have now completed the transaction but have not analyzed why we credited revenue, solely crediting because we debited cash and needed a credit to be in balance. Examining the reasoning behind the behavior of the second account will provide us added security that we have recorded the transaction correctly, and give us a better understanding of how the second account behaves. Revenue has a normal credit balance according to our normal balance cheat sheet, it is going up, and therefore we need to do the same thing to it as its normal balance. We need to credit revenue to make it go up.

It is also useful to note that revenue only goes up. Customers only pay us. We do not pay customers. Net income, revenue minus expenses, will go up and down but revenue will only go in one direction. There are exceptions to this rule but first, learn the rule and we will discuss exceptions in a later text.

Received cash for work completed - $10,000

Accounts	Debit	(Credit)
Cash	10,000	
Revenue or income		(10,000)

Accounts	Beginning Trial Balance	Entries	Ending Trial Balance
Cash	100,000	10,000	110,000
Accounts Receivable	0		0
Supplies	0		0
Accounts Payable	0		0
Unearned Revenue	0		0
Owner Capital	(100,000)		(100,000)
Revenue or income	0	(10,000)	(10,000)
Wages Expense	0	NI	0
Utilities Expense	0		0
Total Debits - Total (cr	0	0	0
Net Income	0	(10,000)	(10,000)

Note the impact of the transaction above, the first column representing the beginning trial balance, the second summarizing our transaction, the third showing the ending trial balance after our transaction. The beginning trial balance, the adjustments, and the ending trial balance all have green zeros in the total debits and credits column representing total debits equaling total credits. The net income has gone up by $10,000 due to revenue going up. Note that the brackets do not represent negative numbers when considering them in terms of debits and credits. The bracketed ($10,000) of net income represents the credit balance of revenue being greater than the debit balance of expenses by ($10,000).

Received cash for work completed - $10,000

Accounts	Debit	(Credit)
Cash	10,000	
Revenue or income		(10,000)

Accounts	Beginning Trial Balance	Entries	Ending Trial Balance
Cash	100,000	10,000	110,000
Accounts Receivable	0		
Supplies	0		
Accounts Payable	0		
Unearned Revenue	0		
Owner Capital	(100,000)		
Revenue or income	0	(10,000)	(10,000)
Wages Expense	0		
Utilities Expense	0		
Total Debits - Total (cr	0		
Net Income	0		

The effect on the accounting equation is assets going up because cash is going up, liabilities remaining the same, and equity going up because revenue is going up and revenue is part of equity.

Next transaction is the business paying employees' wages of $600

Accounts	Beginning Trial Balance
Cash	110,000
Accounts Receivable	0
Supplies	0
Accounts Payable	0
Unearned Revenue	0
Owner Capital	(100,000)
Revenue or income	(10,000)
Wages Expense	0
Utilities Expense	0
Total Debits - Total (cr	0
Net Income	(10,000)

Asking our first question in our thought process; is cash affected, we see that cash is affected, the company paying cash to employees and therefore cash is going down for the company, so we will **write this part of the journal entry down**. Cash is an asset with a normal balance of a debit so we need to do the opposite thing to it to make cash go down, which is a credit. Note that the credit will go on the bottom and we want to leave room for the debit to go on top. The credit going on the bottom of transactions is just tradition, a convention. In other words, putting the credit on top would not make the journal entry wrong or unworkable but would make it formatted in an unconventional way, and we want to follow convention unless, and until, we have a reason to depart from standard convention.

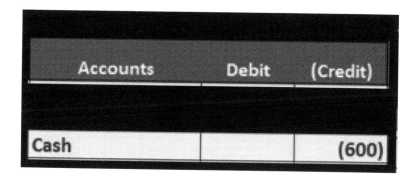

Accounts	Debit	(Credit)
Cash		(600)

If there is only one other account affected we know that we must be debating it by 600 so that the total debits will equal total credits, so we will **write this down**.

Accounts	Debit	(Credit)
	600	
Cash		(600)

Now we just need to determine which other account is affected in this transaction. If we paid employees to help generate revenue the second account would be, wages expense, so we will **write this down**.

Accounts	Debit	(Credit)
Wages Expense	600	
Cash		(600)

The journal entry is now complete, but we have not analyzed why we are debiting wages expense, only debiting based on cash being credited. All expense accounts will have debit balances and according to our normal balance cheat sheet, we need to do the same thing to an account to make it go up. Therefore, we need to debit wages expense to increase wages expense.

It's also useful to know that expense accounts only generally go up in the debit direction. For example, the business only pays employees and employees never pay the company. There will be exceptions to this rule, which we will cover in a later text, but for now, we can depend on the rule that expenses will only be debited and never credited.

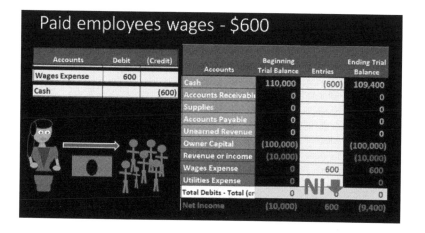

Paid employees wages - $600

Accounts	Debit	(Credit)
Wages Expense	600	
Cash		(600)

Accounts	Beginning Trial Balance	Entries	Ending Trial Balance
Cash	110,000	(600)	109,400
Accounts Receivable	0		0
Supplies	0		0
Accounts Payable	0		0
Unearned Revenue	0		0
Owner Capital	(100,000)		(100,000)
Revenue or Income	(10,000)		(10,000)
Wages Expense	0	600	600
Utilities Expense	0		0
Total Debits - Total (cr	0		0
Net Income	(10,000)	600	(9,400)

Note the impact of the transaction above, the first column representing the beginning trial balance, the second summarizing our transaction, the third showing the ending trial balance after our transaction. The beginning trial balance, the adjustments, and the ending trial balance all have green zeros in the total debits and credits row representing total debits equaling total credits. The net income has gone down by $600 because expenses went up which brings net income down. Net income is now $9,400 calculated as revenue of $10,000 minus expenses of $600.

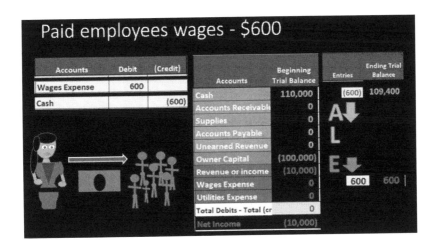

Paid employees wages - $600

Accounts	Debit	(Credit)
Wages Expense	600	
Cash		(600)

Accounts	Beginning Trial Balance	Entries	Ending Trial Balance
Cash	110,000	(600)	109,400
Accounts Receivable	0		
Supplies	0		
Accounts Payable	0		
Unearned Revenue	0		
Owner Capital	(100,000)		
Revenue or income	(10,000)		
Wages Expense	0	600	600
Utilities Expense	0		
Total Debits - Total (cr	0		
Net Income	(10,000)		

The accounting equation is affected by assets going down due to cash going down, liabilities remaining the same, and equity going down due to expenses going up, expenses being part of total equity. The relation between expenses and equity can be confusing because expenses increasing will bring down total equity. The reason expenses bring down equity is because they have a debit balance, a debit balance being the opposite of the net equity normal balance.

We can also think of expenses as decreasing net income and net income being part of total equity. When net income goes up, equity goes up, and when net income goes down equity goes down. Expenses bring net income down and therefore bring total equity down.

Next transaction is the business receiving cash of $15,000 for work that will be done in the future.

Accounts	Beginning Trial Balance
Cash	109,400
Accounts Receivable	0
Supplies	0
Accounts Payable	0
Unearned Revenue	0
Owner Capital	(100,000)
Revenue or income	(10,000)
Wages Expense	600
Utilities Expense	0
Total Debits - Total (cr	0
Net Income	(9,400)

Asking our first question in our thought process; is cash affected, we see that cash is affected, the company receiving cash to for work that has not yet been done and therefore, cash is going up for the company, so we will **write this part of the journal entry down**. Cash is an asset with a normal balance of a debit so we need to do the same thing to it to make cash go up, which is a debit.

Accounts	Debit	(Credit)
Cash	15,000	

If there is only one other account affected we know that we must be crediting it by $15,000 so that the total debits will equal total credits, so we will **write this down**.

Accounts	Debit	(Credit)
Cash	15,000	
		(15,000)

Now we just need to determine which other account is affected by this transaction. Determining the second account in this transaction can be a little tricky. When we receive money from a customer, we usually consider the credit to be revenue, but the revenue has not yet been earned in this case, the work not yet having been done. According to the revenue recognition principle, we cannot recognize revenue until it is earned. Therefore, we will credit unearned revenue, a liability account representing the fact that we owe something in the future, that we owe our services in the future. Note that most businesses receive money after they do work or at the same time the work is done, but some businesses collect cash before work is done. For example, a newspaper company will generally collect cash before earning revenue by delivering newspapers. A rental company collecting a security deposit on the property rented is a kind of unearned revenue, the money received not representing income but a liability, something owed back at the end of the lease or something earned over time.

Accounts	Debit	(Credit)
Cash	15,000	
Unearned Revenue		(15,000)

The journal entry is now complete but we have not analyzed why we are crediting unearned revenue, only crediting based on cash being debited. Unearned revenue is a liability account, as we can see on the trial balance, indicated by it being grouped next to other liabilities like accounts payable. Liabilities have a normal credit balance according to our normal balance cheat sheet and we need to make it go up by doing the same thing to it as its normal balance. Therefore, we need to credit unearned revenue to make it go up.

Received cash for work that will be done in the future - $15,000.

Accounts	Debit	(Credit)
Cash	15,000	
Unearned Revenue		(15,000)

Accounts	Beginning Trial Balance	Entries	Ending Trial Balance
Cash	109,400	15,000	124,400
Accounts Receivable	0		0
Supplies	0		0
Accounts Payable	0		0
Unearned Revenue	0	(15,000)	(15,000)
Owner Capital	(100,000)		(100,000)
Revenue or Income	(10,000)		(10,000)
Wages Expense	600		600
Utilities Expense	0		0
Total Debits - Total (cr	0	0	0
Net Income	(9,400)	0	(9,400)

Note the impact of the transaction above, the first column representing the beginning trial balance, the second summarizing our transaction, the third showing the ending trial balance after our transaction. The beginning trial balance, the adjustments, and the ending trial balance all have green zeros in the total debits and credits row representing total debits equaling total credits.

Next transaction is the business paying cash of $750 for the utility bill.

Accounts	Beginning Trial Balance
Cash	124,400
Accounts Receivable	0
Supplies	0
Accounts Payable	0
Unearned Revenue	(15,000)
Owner Capital	(100,000)
Revenue or income	(10,000)
Wages Expense	600
Utilities Expense	0
Total Debits - Total (cr	0
Net Income	(9,400)

Asking our first question in our thought process; is cash affected, we see that cash is affected the company paying cash for utilities and therefore cash is going down for the company, so we **will write this part of the journal entry down**. Cash is an asset with a normal balance of a debit so we need to do the opposite thing to it to make cash go down, which is a credit. Note that the credit will go on the bottom of the journal entry and we want to leave room for the debit to go on top. The credit going on the bottom of transactions is just tradition, a convention. In other words, putting the credit on top would not make the journal entry wrong or unworkable, but would make it formatted in an unconventional way, and we want to follow convention unless there is justification for deviating from it.

Accounts	Debit	(Credit)
Cash		(750)

If there is only one other account affected we know that we must be debating it by $750 so that the total debits will equal total credits, so we will **write this down**.

Accounts	Debit	(Credit)
	750	
Cash		(750)

Now we just need to determine which other account is affected by this transaction. If we paid the utility bill the second account would be utility expense, so we will **write this down**.

Accounts	Debit	(Credit)
Utilities Expense	750	
Cash		(750)

The journal entry is now complete but we have not analyzed why we are debiting utility expense, only debiting based on cash being credited. All expense accounts will have debit balances and according to our normal balance cheat sheet, we need to do the same thing to an account to make it go up. Therefore, we need to debit utility expense to increase utility expense. It's also useful to know that expense accounts only generally go up in the debit direction. For example, the business only pays the utility company and the utility company never pays the business. There will be exceptions to this rule, which we will cover in a later text, but for now, we can depend on the rule that expenses will only be debited and never credited.

Paid cash for utilities - $750.

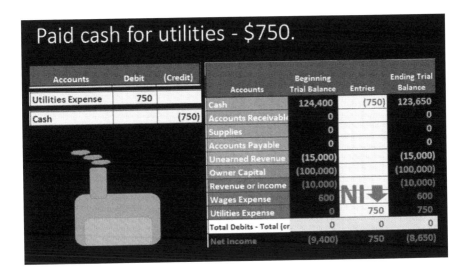

Accounts	Debit	(Credit)
Utilities Expense	750	
Cash		(750)

Accounts	Beginning Trial Balance	Entries	Ending Trial Balance
Cash	124,400	(750)	123,650
Accounts Receivable	0		0
Supplies	0		0
Accounts Payable	0		0
Unearned Revenue	(15,000)		(15,000)
Owner Capital	(100,000)		(100,000)
Revenue or income	(10,000)		(10,000)
Wages Expense	600		600
Utilities Expense	0	750	750
Total Debits - Total (cr	0	0	0
Net Income	(9,400)	750	(8,650)

Note the impact of the transaction above, the first column representing the beginning trial balance, the second summarizing our transaction, the third showing the ending trial balance after our transaction. The beginning trial balance, the adjustments, and the ending trial balance all have green zeros in the total debits and credits row representing total debits equaling total credits. Net income is $8,650 calculated as revenue of $10,000 minus wages expenses of $600 and utility expenses of $750.

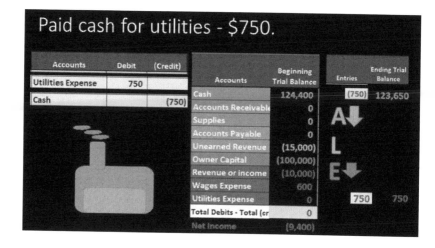

Paid cash for utilities - $750.

Accounts	Debit	(Credit)
Utilities Expense	750	
Cash		(750)

Accounts	Beginning Trial Balance	Entries	Ending Trial Balance
Cash	124,400	(750)	123,650
Accounts Receivable	0		
Supplies	0		
Accounts Payable	0		
Unearned Revenue	(15,000)		
Owner Capital	(100,000)		
Revenue or income	(10,000)		
Wages Expense	600		
Utilities Expense	0	750	750
Total Debits - Total (cr	0		
Net Income	(9,400)		

The accounting equation is affected by assets going down due to cash going down, liabilities remaining the same, and equity going down due to expenses going up, expenses being part of total equity. The relation between expenses and equity can be confusing because expenses increasing will bring dôwn total equity. The reason expenses bring down equity is because they have a debit balance, a debit balance being the opposite of the net equity normal balance. We can also think of expenses as decreasing net income and net income being part of total equity. When net income goes up, equity goes up, and when net income goes down, equity goes down. Expenses bring net income down and therefore bring total equity down.

Next transaction is the business paying cash of $350 for supplies.

Accounts	Beginning Trial Balance
Cash	123,650
Accounts Receivable	0
Supplies	0
Accounts Payable	0
Unearned Revenue	(15,000)
Owner Capital	(100,000)
Revenue or income	(10,000)
Wages Expense	600
Utilities Expense	750
Total Debits - Total (cr	0
Net Income	(8,650)

Asking our first question in our thought process; is cash affected, we see that cash is affected, the company paying cash for supplies and therefore cash is going down for the company, so we will **write this part of the journal entry down**. Cash is an asset with a normal balance of a debit so we need to do the opposite thing to it to make cash go down, which is a credit. Note that the credit will go on the bottom of the journal entry and we want to leave room for the debit to go on top. The credit going on the bottom of transactions is just tradition, a convention. In other words, putting the credit on top would not make the journal entry wrong or unworkable but would make it formatted in an unconventional way.

Accounts	Debit	(Credit)
Cash		(350)

If there is only one other account affected we know that we must be debating it by $350 so that the total debits will equal total credits, so we will **write this down**.

Accounts	Debit	(Credit)
	350	
Cash		(350)

Now we just need to determine which other account is affected in this transaction. If we paid for supplies the second account would be the account called, supplies. Note that we will be recording to an asset account called supplies rather than an expense account because supplies are something that has not yet been consumed by the business to help generate revenue. Supplies will first be recorded an asset and then moved to an expense as the supplies are used.

Note the purchase of a few supplies may just be expensed at the time of purchase because the amount is not material to decision making, and expensing at the time of purchase is less work. Recording supplies as an asset will also introduce us to ideas related to tracking inventory because the tracking of the physical units of supplies will be similar to tracking the physical units of inventory.

Accounts	Debit	(Credit)
Supplies	350	
Cash		(350)

The journal entry is now complete, but we have not analyzed why we are debiting supplies, only debiting based on cash being credited. Asset accounts will have debit balances and according to our normal balance cheat sheet, we need to do the same thing to an account to make it go up. Therefore, we need to debit supplies to increase the supplies account.

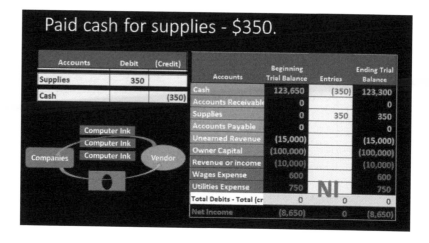

Paid cash for supplies - $350.

Accounts	Debit	(Credit)
Supplies	350	
Cash		(350)

Accounts	Beginning Trial Balance	Entries	Ending Trial Balance
Cash	123,650	(350)	123,300
Accounts Receivable	0		0
Supplies	0	350	350
Accounts Payable	0		0
Unearned Revenue	(15,000)		(15,000)
Owner Capital	(100,000)		(100,000)
Revenue or income	(10,000)		(10,000)
Wages Expense	600		600
Utilities Expense	750		750
Total Debits - Total (cr	0	0	0
Net Income	(8,650)	0	(8,650)

Note the impact of the transaction above, the first column representing the beginning trial balance, the second summarizing our transaction, the third showing the ending trial balance after our transaction. The beginning trial balance, the adjustments, and the ending trial balance all have green zeros in the total debits and credits row representing total debits equaling total credits. Net income is not affected by this transaction, the transaction resulting in one asset going down and one asset going up, the asset of cash going down and the asset of supplies going up.

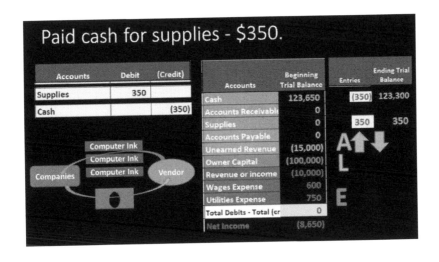

Paid cash for supplies - $350.

Accounts	Debit	(Credit)
Supplies	350	
Cash		(350)

Accounts	Beginning Trial Balance	Entries	Ending Trial Balance
Cash	123,650	(350)	123,300
Accounts Receivable	0		
Supplies	0	350	350
Accounts Payable	0		
Unearned Revenue	(15,000)		
Owner Capital	(100,000)		
Revenue or income	(10,000)		
Wages Expense	600		
Utilities Expense	750		
Total Debits - Total (cr	0		
Net Income	(8,650)		

The accounting equation is affected by assets going down due to cash going down but also going up due to supplies going up, the result being no effect on total asset nor any part of the accounting equation, liabilities remaining the same and equity remaining the same

Ch. 16 Recording Transactions for the Accounts Receivable or Revenue Cycle

Now that we have seen many transactions that include cash as one component we will record transactions related to a typical accounts receivable, or revenue cycle, one where work is done, an invoice is made, and cash is received later. Cash will still be included in some of the transactions related to the accounts receivable, or revenue, cycle but will not be included in every transaction.

In the first transaction work is completed and an invoice is sent for $10,000

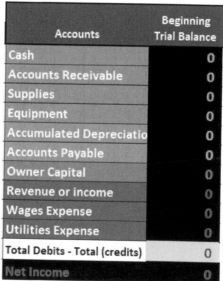

Accounts	Beginning Trial Balance
Cash	0
Accounts Receivable	0
Supplies	0
Equipment	0
Accumulated Depreciatio	0
Accounts Payable	0
Owner Capital	0
Revenue or income	0
Wages Expense	0
Utilities Expense	0
Total Debits - Total (credits)	0
Net Income	0

Asking our first question in our thought process; is cash affected? The answer is no. Cash is not involved in this transaction, although we hope to receive cash at some point in the future. If cash is not affected, we will focus first on what the company received. The company has received a promise of payment based on the agreement between the buyer and seller. The work has been completed, and therefore the company is owed the money related to the job, this being an asset record in the account of account receivable. Recording an asset that does not represent something tangible, something we have not physically received, can seem unusual but the receivable does have value and is useful information for both internal decision making and to external users of financial statements. For example, a bank assessing whether to give a company a loan would want to know if there are outstanding receivables because this could make the repayment of the loan more likely.

Accounts receivable is an asset. Assets have normal debit balances according to our normal balance cheat sheet. Therefore, we will do the same thing as the normal balance to make the asset go up, debiting the asset account.

Accounts	Debit	(Credit)
Accounts Receivable	10,000	

If there is only one other account affected we know that we

must be crediting it by $10,000 so that the total debits will equal total

credits, so we will **write this down**.

Accounts	Debit	(Credit)
Accounts Receivable	10,000	
		(10,000)

Now we just need to determine which other account is affected

by this transaction. The reason customers owe us money in the future is

that we completed work and therefore revenue will be the account

credited. Under the revenue recognition principle, we record revenue

when the work is done.

Accounts	Debit	(Credit)
Accounts Receivable	10,000	
Revenue or income		(10,000)

The journal entry is now complete, but we have not analyzed

why we are crediting revenue, only crediting based on accounts

receivable being debited. Revenue has a normal credit balance

according to our normal balance cheat sheet, and it is going up.

Therefore, we need to do the same thing to it as its normal balance. We need to credit revenue to make it go up. It is also useful to note that revenue only goes up, customers only paying us. We do not pay customers. Net income, revenue minus expenses, will go up and down but revenue will only go in one direction. There are exceptions to this rule but first, learn the rule, and we will discuss exceptions in a later text.

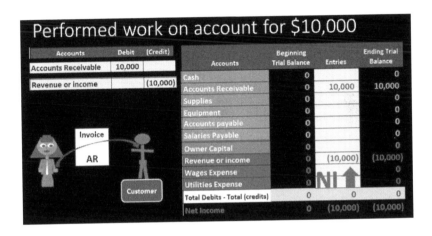

Note the impact of this transaction above, the first column representing the beginning trial balance, the second summarizing our transaction, the third showing the ending trial balance after our transaction. The beginning trial balance, the adjustments, and the ending trial balance all have green zeros in the total debits and credits row representing total debits equaling total credits. Net income is going up because revenue is going up by $10,000. Note that the brackets do not represent a negative number when seen through the lens of debits and credits. The brackets represent credits.

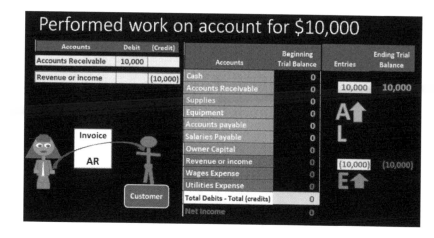

Performed work on account for $10,000

Accounts	Debit	(Credit)
Accounts Receivable	10,000	
Revenue or income		(10,000)

Accounts	Beginning Trial Balance	Entries	Ending Trial Balance
Cash	0		
Accounts Receivable	0	10,000	10,000
Supplies	0		
Equipment	0		
Accounts payable	0		
Salaries Payable	0		
Owner Capital	0		
Revenue or income	0	(10,000)	(10,000)
Wages Expense	0		
Utilities Expense	0		
Total Debits - Total (credits)	0		
Net Income	0		

The accounting equation is affected by assets going up due to accounts receivable going up, liabilities remaining the same, and equity going up due to revenue going up, income statement accounts of revenue and expenses being part of the equity section in the accounting equation.

In the second transaction cash is received for work completed in the past for $10,000

Accounts	Beginning Trial Balance
Cash	0
Accounts Receivable	10,000
Supplies	0
Equipment	0
Accumulated Depreciatio	0
Accounts Payable	0
Owner Capital	0
Revenue or income	(10,000)
Wages Expense	0
Utilities Expense	0
Total Debits - Total (credits)	0
Net Income	(10,000)

Asking our first question in our thought process; is cash affected; the answer is yes. Cash has been received so we will **write this down**. Cash is an asset. Assets have normal debit balances. Therefore, to make cash go up, we will do the same thing as the normal balance and debit cash.

Accounts	Debit	(Credit)
Cash	10,000	

If there is only one other account affected we know that we must be crediting it by $10,000 so that the total debits will equal total credits, so we will **write this down**.

Accounts	Debit	(Credit)
Cash	10,000	
		(10,000)

Now we just need to determine which other account is affected by this transaction. The reason we received cash from customers is that we did work, which may lead us to credit revenue, but the work had been done in the past. The revenue related to this $10,000 received has already been recorded, and an asset account of accounts receivable had been recorded at the time the work was done. We now need to reduce the asset account of accounts receivable, representing the fact that the customer no longer owes the company money.

Accounts	Debit	(Credit)
Cash	10,000	
Accounts Receivable		(10,000)

The journal entry is now complete, but we have not analyzed why we are crediting accounts receivable, only crediting based on cash being debited. Accounts receivable has a normal debit balance according to our normal balance cheat sheet, and it is going down because the customer no longer owes the company money after they have paid. Therefore, we need to do the opposite thing to it as its

normal balance. We need to credit accounts receivable to make it go

down.

Received cash on account - $10,000

Accounts	Debit	(Credit)		Accounts	Beginning Trial Balance	Entries	Ending Trial Balance
Cash	10,000			Cash	0	10,000	10,000
Accounts Receivable		(10,000)		Accounts Receivable	10,000	(10,000)	0
				Supplies	0		0
				Equipment	0		0
				Accounts payable	0		0
				Salaries Payable	0		0
				Owner Capital	0		0
				Revenue or income	(10,000)		(10,000)
				Wages Expense	0		0
				Utilities Expense	0		0
				Total Debits - Total (credits)	0	0	0
				Net Income	(10,000)	0	(10,000)

Note the impact of the transaction above, the first column

representing the beginning trial balance, the second summarizing our

transaction, the third showing the ending trial balance after our

transaction. The beginning trial balance, the adjustments, and the

ending trial balance all have green zeros in the total debits and credits

row representing total debits equaling total credits. Net income is not

affected even though cash is received because income had been

recorded at the time work was done.

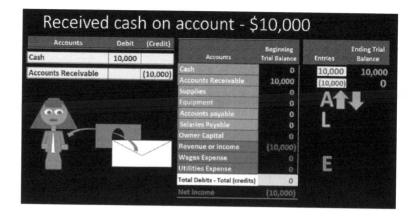

Received cash on account - $10,000

Accounts	Debit	(Credit)
Cash	10,000	
Accounts Receivable		(10,000)

Accounts	Beginning Trial Balance	Entries	Ending Trial Balance
Cash	0	10,000	10,000
Accounts Receivable	10,000	(10,000)	0
Supplies	0		
Equipment	0		
Accounts payable	0		
Salaries Payable	0		
Owner Capital	0		
Revenue or income	(10,000)		
Wages Expense	0		
Utilities Expense	0		
Total Debits - Total (credits)	0		
Net Income	(10,000)		

The accounting equation is affected by assets going up due to cash going up but asset also going down due to accounts receivable going down. The company has gained one asset and lost another. Therefore, there is no effect on the accounting equation. Assets, liabilities, and equity remain the same.

The accounts receivable or revenue cycle can be very complex, requiring the tracking of many customer accounts, but the transactions above show the essence of the accounts receivable cycle. The accounts receivable cycle will include sales made on account, meaning cash has not yet been received for work done. Amounts owed are then tracked in the accounts receivable account, followed by the receipt of cash from customers at a future date. At the time cash is received the accounts receivable account is reduced.

Ch. 17 Recording Transactions for the Accounts Payable Cycle

Most companies have an accounts payable cycle, a series of transactions starting with purchases on account, followed by payments at a later date. Analyzing transactions specific to this cycle helps structure the learning of transactions in smaller, more manageable, chunks.

In the first transaction, the company purchases supplies on account for $450

Accounts	Beg Trial Balance
Cash	50,000
Accounts Receivable	0
Supplies	0
Accounts Payable	0
Owner Capital	(40,000)
Revenue or income	(10,000)
Wages Expense	0
Utilities Expense	0
Meals and Ent. Expense	0
Auto Expense	0
Total Debits - Total (credits)	0
Net Income	(10,000)

Asking our first question in our thought process; is cash affected? The answer is no. Cash is not involved in this transaction, although cash will need to be paid at some point in the future. If cash is not affected, we will focus first on what the company received. The company has received supplies in this transaction. Supplies are asset type accounts. Assets have normal debit balance according to our normal balance cheat sheet. Therefore, we will do the same thing as the normal balance to make the asset go up, debiting the asset account.

Accounts	Debit	(Credit)
Supplies	450	

If there is only one other account affected we know that we must be crediting it by $450 so that the total debits will equal total credits, so we will **write this down**.

Accounts	Debit	(Credit)
Supplies	450	
		(450)

Now we just need to determine which other account is affected by this transaction. Because we did not pay cash the credit will not be to the cash account. Instead, the credited account will be to a liability account called account payable.

Accounts	Debit	(Credit)
Supplies	450	
Accounts Payable		(450)

The journal entry is now complete, but we have not analyzed why we are crediting accounts payable, only crediting based on supplies being debited. Accounts payable has a normal credit balance according to our normal balance cheat sheet, and it is going up because the company owes more money after this transaction. Therefore, we need to do the same thing to it as its normal balance. We need to credit accounts payable to make it go up.

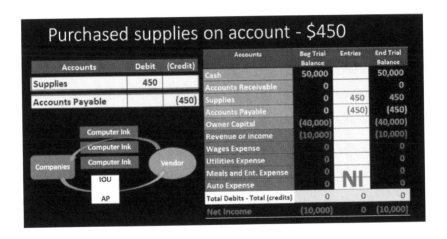

Note the impact of the transaction above, the first column representing the beginning trial balance, the second summarizing our transaction, the third showing the ending trial balance after our transaction. The beginning trial balance, the adjustments, and the ending trial balance all have green zeros in the total debits and credits row representing total debits equaling total credits. Net income is not affected even though we purchased supplies because we have not yet used the supplies to help generate revenue.

Purchased supplies on account - $450

Accounts	Debit	(Credit)
Supplies	450	
Accounts Payable		(450)

Accounts	Beg Trial Balance	
Cash	50,000	**A** ⬆
Accounts Receivable	0	
Supplies	0	450 450
Accounts Payable	0	(450) (450)
Owner Capital	(40,000)	**L** ⬆
Revenue or income	(10,000)	
Wages Expense	0	
Utilities Expense	0	**E**
Meals and Ent. Expense	0	
Auto Expense	0	
Total Debits - Total (credits)	0	
Net Income	(10,000)	

Computer Ink, Computer Ink, Computer Ink, Companies, Vendor, IOU, AP

The accounting equation is affected by assets going up due to supplies going up, liabilities going up due to accounts payable going up, and equity staying the same.

In the second transaction, the company pays cash for purchase made in the past of $450

Accounts	Beg Trial Balance
Cash	50,000
Accounts Receivable	0
Supplies	450
Accounts Payable	(450)
Owner Capital	(40,000)
Revenue or income	(10,000)
Wages Expense	0
Utilities Expense	0
Meals and Ent. Expense	0
Auto Expense	0
Total Debits - Total (credits)	0
Net Income	(10,000)

Asking our first question in our thought process; is cash affected? The answer is yes. Cash has been paid and therefore, is going down, so we will **write this down**. Cash is an asset. Assets have normal

debit balances. Therefore, we will credit cash to make it go down.

Accounts	Debit	(Credit)
Cash		(450)

If there is only one other account affected we know that we

must be debiting it by $450 so that the total debits will equal total

credits, so we will **write this down**.

Accounts	Debit	(Credit)
	450	
Cash		(450)

Now we just need to determine which other account is affected

by this transaction. The reason we are paying cash is for the supplies we

purchased in the past, but we will not be debiting the supplies account

because supplies were already recorded at the point of purchase even

though cash was not paid. Instead, we will debit accounts payable,

reducing the liability we owe.

Accounts	Debit	(Credit)
Accounts Payable	450	
Cash		(450)

The journal entry is now complete, but we have not analyzed why we are debiting accounts payable, only debiting based on cash being credited. Accounts payable has a normal credit balance according to our normal balance cheat sheet, and it is going down because the company owes less money after this transaction. Therefore, we need to do the opposite thing to it as its normal balance. We need to debit accounts payable to make it go down.

Paid cash for supplies purchased on account - $450

Accounts	Debit	(Credit)
Accounts Payable	450	
Cash		(450)

Accounts	Beg Trial Balance	Entries	End Trial Balance
Cash	50,000	(450)	49,550
Accounts Receivable	0		0
Supplies	450		450
Accounts Payable	(450)	450	0
Owner Capital	(40,000)		(40,000)
Revenue or income	(10,000)		(10,000)
Wages Expense	0		0
Utilities Expense	0		0
Meals and Ent. Expense	0	NI	0
Auto Expense	0		0
Total Debits - Total (credits)	0	0	0
Net Income	(10,000)	0	(10,000)

Note the impact of the transaction above, the first column representing the beginning trial balance, the second summarizing our transaction, the third showing the ending trial balance after our transaction. The beginning trial balance, the adjustments, and the ending trial balance all have green zeros in the total debits and credits

row representing total debits equaling total credits. Net income is not

affected even though we paid cash because the cash payment was

made to reduce a liability. Under accrual accounting supplies will not be

expensed at the time of purchase or the time of payment, but at the

date of use, at the date of consumption.

Paid cash for supplies purchased on account - $450

Accounts	Debit	(Credit)
Accounts Payable	450	
Cash		(450)

Accounts	Beg Trial Balance		
Cash	50,000	(450)	49,550
Accounts Receivable	0		
Supplies	450		
Accounts Payable	(450)	450	0
Owner Capital	(40,000)		
Revenue or income	(10,000)		
Wages Expense	0		
Utilities Expense	0		
Meals and Ent. Expense	0		
Auto Expense	0		
Total Debits - Total (credits)	0		
Net Income	(10,000)		

Mail Box

A L E

The accounting equation is affected by assets going down due

to cash going down, liabilities going down due to accounts payable

going down, and equity staying the same.

The accounts payable cycle can be very complex, involving many

transactions, and many accounts that need to be tracked and paid but

the two transactions above represent the essence of the cycle. The

accounts payable cycle will involve purchases made on account,

meaning no cash was paid at the time of purchase. The amount owed will be tracked in the accounts payable account until payment. When payment is made the accounts payable account will be reduced because the company no longer owes money on this account.

Ch. 18 Transactions by Date Comprehensive Problem

Now that we have seen cash transactions and transactions related to the accounts receivable and accounts payable cycle, we will look at transactions in order by date, using a comprehensive problem. We will generate the journal entries, post the transactions to the general ledger, and use the general ledger to create the trial balance after each transaction.

Below is the chart of accounts we will be using. The order of the chart of accounts is assets, liabilities, equity, revenue, and expenses.

Accounts
Cash-Checking
Accounts Receivable
Landscaping Supplies
Prepaid insurance
Auto
Acc. Depr. - Auto
Lawn Equipment
Acc. Depr. - Lawn Equipment
Accounts Payable
Notes payable
Interest Payable
Unearned Revenue
Capital
Drawing
Revenue
Landscaping Supplies Expense
Auto Expense
Advertising Expense
Equipment Rental Expense
Insurance Expense
Depreciation Expense - Auto
Depreciation Expense - Lawn E
Interest Expense

1) **7/1 Owner deposits money into the business bank account of $3,000**

Cash is affected and is going up with a debit. The other account affected is capital which must then be credited. Capital is a credit balance account and needs to go up. Therefore, we do the same thing

to it of another credit.

7/1	Cash-Checking	3,000	
	Capital		(3,000)

The transaction is then posted to the general ledger.

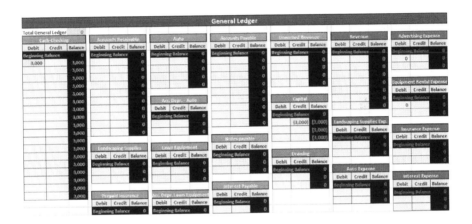

The trial balance is constructed from the general ledger. Note

that the ending balances on the general ledger are what comprise the

balances in the trial balance.

Accounts	Trial Balance
Cash-Checking	3,000
Accounts Receivable	0
Landscaping Supplies	0
Prepaid insurance	0
Auto	0
Acc. Depr. - Auto	0
Lawn Equipment	0
Acc. Depr. - Lawn Equipment	0
Accounts Payable	0
Notes payable	0
Interest Payable	0
Unearned Revenue	0
Capital	(3,000)
Drawing	0
Revenue	0
Landscaping Supplies Expense	0
Auto Expense	0
Advertising Expense	0
Equipment Rental Expense	0
Insurance Expense	0
Depreciation Expense - Auto	0
Depreciation Expense - Lawn E	0
Interest Expense	0
Total Debits - Total (credits)	0
Net Income	0

2) **7/1 borrows from the bank $8,000**

Cash is affected and is going up with a debit. The other account must then be credited. The other account is a liability of notes payable. Liabilities have normal credit balances and therefore need the same thing as the normal credit balance to make it go up.

7/1	Cash-Checking	8,000	
	Notes payable		(8,000)

The transaction is then posted to the general ledger.

General Ledger

The trial balance is constructed from the general ledger. Note that the ending balances on the general ledger are what comprise the balances in the trial balance.

Accounts	Trial Balance
Cash-Checking	11,000
Accounts Receivable	0
Landscaping Supplies	0
Prepaid insurance	0
Auto	0
Acc. Depr. - Auto	0
Lawn Equipment	0
Acc. Depr. - Lawn Equipment	0
Accounts Payable	0
Notes payable	(8,000)
Interest Payable	0
Unearned Revenue	0
Capital	(3,000)
Drawing	0
Revenue	0
Landscaping Supplies Expense	0
Auto Expense	0
Advertising Expense	0
Equipment Rental Expense	0
Insurance Expense	0
Depreciation Expense - Auto	0
Depreciation Expense - Lawn E	0
Interest Expense	0
Total Debits - Total (credits)	0
Net Income	0

3) 7/5 purchased a truck for cash of $5,000

Cash is affected and is going down with a credit. The other account must
then be debited so the journal entry remains in balance. The second
account will be auto. Auto is an asset account. Assets have normal debit
balances, and therefore, we debit auto to make it go up.

7/5	Auto	5,000	
	Cash-Checking		(5,000)

The transaction is then posted to the general ledger.

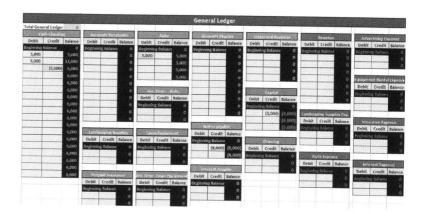

The trial balance is constructed from the general ledger. Note
that the ending balances on the general ledger are what comprise the
balances in the trial balance.

Accounts	Trial Balance
Cash-Checking	6,000
Accounts Receivable	0
Landscaping Supplies	0
Prepaid insurance	0
Auto	5,000
Acc. Depr. - Auto	0
Lawn Equipment	0
Acc. Depr. - Lawn Equipment	0
Accounts Payable	0
Notes payable	(8,000)
Interest Payable	0
Unearned Revenue	0
Capital	(3,000)
Drawing	0
Revenue	0
Landscaping Supplies Expense	0
Auto Expense	0
Advertising Expense	0
Equipment Rental Expense	0
Insurance Expense	0
Depreciation Expense - Auto	0
Depreciation Expense - Lawn E	0
Interest Expense	0
Total Debits - Total (credits)	0
Net Income	0

4) 7/5 Purchase lawn mower and garden tools on account $1,500

Cash is not affected. What we received is lawn equipment. Lawn equipment is an asset and will go up with a debit balance. The second account must then be credited. The second account is accounts payable, a liability account. Liability accounts have normal credit balances and therefore the same thing as the normal balance of another credit will make it go up.

7/5	Lawn Equipment	1,500	
	Accounts Payable		(1,500)

The transaction is then posted to the general ledger.

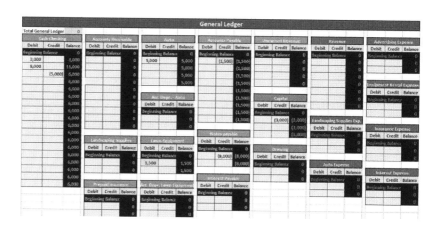

The trial balance is constructed from the general ledger. Note that the ending balances on the general ledger are what comprise the balances in the trial balance.

Accounts	Trial Balance
Cash-Checking	6,000
Accounts Receivable	0
Landscaping Supplies	0
Prepaid Insurance	0
Auto	5,000
Acc. Depr. - Auto	0
Lawn Equipment	1,500
Acc. Depr. - Lawn Equipment	0
Accounts Payable	(1,500)
Notes payable	(8,000)
Interest Payable	0
Unearned Revenue	0
Capital	(3,000)
Drawing	0
Revenue	0
Landscaping Supplies Expense	0
Auto Expense	0
Advertising Expense	0
Equipment Rental Expense	0
Insurance Expense	0
Depreciation Expense - Auto	0
Depreciation Expense - Lawn E	0
Interest Expense	0
Total Debits - Total (credits)	0
Net Income	0

5) 7/6 Purchase landscaping supplies on account for $185

Cash is not affected. What we received are landscaping supplies. Landscaping supplies is an asset and will go up with a debit balance. The second account must then be credited. The second account is accounts payable, a liability account. Liability accounts have normal credit balances and therefore the same thing as the normal balance of another credit will make it go up.

7/6	Landscaping Supplies	185	
	Accounts Payable		(185)

The transaction is then posted to the general ledger.

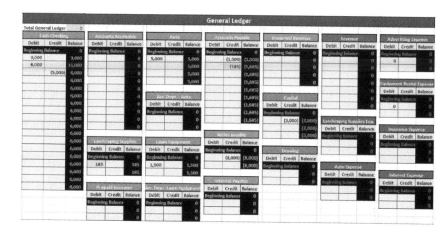

The trial balance is constructed from the general ledger. Note that the ending balances on the general ledger are what comprise the balances in the trial balance.

Accounts	Trial Balance
Cash-Checking	6,000
Accounts Receivable	0
Landscaping Supplies	185
Prepaid insurance	0
Auto	5,000
Acc. Depr. - Auto	0
Lawn Equipment	1,500
Acc. Depr. - Lawn Equipment	0
Accounts Payable	(1,685)
Notes payable	(8,000)
Interest Payable	0
Unearned Revenue	0
Capital	(3,000)
Drawing	0
Revenue	0
Landscaping Supplies Expense	0
Auto Expense	0
Advertising Expense	0
Equipment Rental Expense	0
Insurance Expense	0
Depreciation Expense - Auto	0
Depreciation Expense - Lawn E	0
Interest Expense	0
Total Debits - Total (credits)	0
Net Income	0

6) **7/8 Paid cash for gas and oil if $80**

Cash is affected and is going down with a credit. The other account must then be debited. The second account is auto expense. The auto expense has a normal debit balance and will go up by doing the same thing to it of another debit. Expenses generally only go up in the debit direction.

7/8	Auto Expense	80	
	Cash-Checking		(80)

The transaction is then posted to the general ledger.

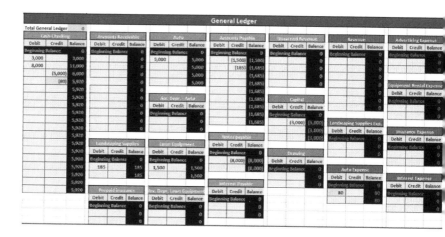

The trial balance is constructed from the general ledger. Note that the ending balances on the general ledger are what comprise the balances in the trial balance.

Accounts	Trial Balance
Cash-Checking	5,920
Accounts Receivable	0
Landscaping Supplies	185
Prepaid insurance	0
Auto	5,000
Acc. Depr. - Auto	0
Lawn Equipment	1,500
Acc. Depr. - Lawn Equipment	0
Accounts Payable	(1,685)
Notes payable	(8,000)
Interest Payable	0
Unearned Revenue	0
Capital	(3,000)
Drawing	0
Revenue	0
Landscaping Supplies Expense	0
Auto Expense	80
Advertising Expense	0
Equipment Rental Expense	0
Insurance Expense	0
Depreciation Expense - Auto	0
Depreciation Expense - Lawn E	0
Interest Expense	0
Total Debits - Total (credits)	0
Net Income	80

7) **7/8 Purchased advertising on account for $315**

Cash is not affected. The business received advertising.

Advertising expense is an expense account with a normal debit balance

and therefore the same thing of another debit will make it go up. The

second account must then be credited. The second account is accounts

payable, a liability account, liability accounts having a normal balance of

a credit and needing the same thing of another credit to go up.

7/8	Advertising Expense	315	
	Accounts Payable		(315)

The transaction is then posted to the general ledger.

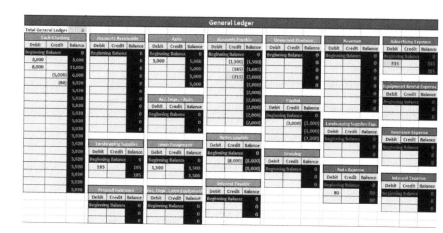

The trial balance is constructed from the general ledger. Note that the ending balances on the general ledger are what comprise the balances in the trial balance.

Accounts	Trial Balance
Cash-Checking	5,920
Accounts Receivable	0
Landscaping Supplies	185
Prepaid insurance	0
Auto	5,000
Acc. Depr. - Auto	0
Lawn Equipment	1,500
Acc. Depr. - Lawn Equipment	0
Accounts Payable	(2,000)
Notes payable	(8,000)
Interest Payable	0
Unearned Revenue	0
Capital	(3,000)
Drawing	0
Revenue	0
Landscaping Supplies Expense	0
Auto Expense	80
Advertising Expense	315
Equipment Rental Expense	0
Insurance Expense	0
Depreciation Expense - Auto	0
Depreciation Expense - Lawn E	0
Interest Expense	0
Total Debits - Total (credits)	0
Net Income	395

8) **7/9 received cash for work that will be done in the future of $360**

Cash is affected and goes up with a debit. The second account must then be credited. The second account is not revenue because we have not yet earned the revenue. Therefore, we must credit the liability account of unearned revenue, unearned revenue going up because we owe something in the future. Liability accounts have normal credit balances and therefore the same thing of another credit will make unearned revenue go up.

7/9	Cash-Checking	360	
	Unearned Revenue		(360)

The transaction is then posted to the general ledger.

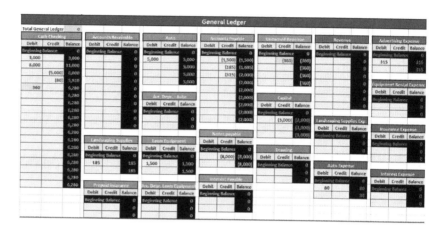

The trial balance is constructed from the general ledger. Note that the ending balances on the general ledger are what comprise the balances in the trial balance.

Accounts	Trial Balance
Cash-Checking	6,280
Accounts Receivable	0
Landscaping Supplies	185
Prepaid insurance	0
Auto	5,000
Acc. Depr. - Auto	0
Lawn Equipment	1,500
Acc. Depr. - Lawn Equipment	0
Accounts Payable	(2,000)
Notes payable	(8,000)
Interest Payable	0
Unearned Revenue	(360)
Capital	(3,000)
Drawing	0
Revenue	0
Landscaping Supplies Expense	0
Auto Expense	80
Advertising Expense	315
Equipment Rental Expense	0
Insurance Expense	0
Depreciation Expense - Auto	0
Depreciation Expense - Lawn E	0
Interest Expense	0
Total Debits - Total (credits)	0
Net Income	395

9) **7/15 paid cash to rent equipment for $75**

Cash is affected and is going down with a credit. The second account must then be debited. The second account is equipment rental expense. Expense accounts have normal debit balances and the same thing will make them go up. Expense accounts generally only go up.

7/15	Equipment Rental Expense	75	
	Cash-Checking		(75)

The transaction is then posted to the general ledger.

General Ledger

Total General Ledger	0

Cash-Checking

Debit	Credit	Balance
Beginning Balance		0
3,000		3,000
8,000		11,000
	(5,000)	6,000
	(80)	5,920
360		6,280
	(75)	6,205
		6,205
		6,205
		6,205
		6,205
		6,205
		6,205
		6,205
		6,205
		6,205
		6,205

Accounts Receivable

Debit	Credit	Balance
Beginning Balance		0
		0
		0
		0
		0
		0
		0
		0

Accounts Payable Discounts

Debit	Credit	Balance
Beginning Balance		0
185	185	
		185

Prepaid Insurance

Debit	Credit	Balance
Beginning Balance		0
		0
		0

Auto

Debit	Credit	Balance
Beginning Balance		0
5,000		5,000
	5,000	
	5,000	
	5,000	

Acc. Depreciation-Auto

Debit	Credit	Balance
Beginning Balance		0
		0

Notes Receivable

Debit	Credit	Balance
Beginning Balance		0
1,500	1,500	
	1,500	

Note-Long Term Receivable

Debit	Credit	Balance
Beginning Balance		0
		0
		0

Accounts Payable

Debit	Credit	Balance
Beginning Balance		0
(1,500)	(1,500)	
(185)	(1,685)	
(315)	(2,000)	
	(2,000)	
	(2,000)	
	(2,000)	
	(2,000)	
	(2,000)	
	(2,000)	

Notes payable

Debit	Credit	Balance
Beginning Balance		0
(8,000)	(8,000)	
	(8,000)	

Interest Payable

Debit	Credit	Balance
Beginning Balance		0
		0
		0

Unearned Revenue

Debit	Credit	Balance
Beginning Balance		0
	(360)	(360)
		(360)
		(360)
		(360)

Capital

Debit	Credit	Balance
Beginning Balance		0
	(3,000)	(3,000)
		(3,000)
		(3,000)

Drawing

Debit	Credit	Balance
Beginning Balance		0
		0

Revenue

Debit	Credit	Balance
Beginning Balance		0
		0
		0
		0
		0
		0

Advertising Expense

Debit	Credit	Balance
Beginning Balance		0
315		315
		315

Equipment Rental Expense

Debit	Credit	Balance
Beginning Balance		0
75		75
		75

Landscaping Supplies Exp.

Debit	Credit	Balance
Beginning Balance		0
		0

Insurance Expense

Debit	Credit	Balance
Beginning Balance		0
		0

Auto Expense

Debit	Credit	Balance
Beginning Balance		0
		0

Interest Expense

Debit	Credit	Balance
Beginning Balance		0
80		80
		80

The trial balance is constructed from the general ledger. Note that the ending balances on the general ledger are what comprise the balances in the trial balance.

Accounts	Trial Balance
Cash-Checking	6,205
Accounts Receivable	0
Landscaping Supplies	185
Prepaid insurance	0
Auto	5,000
Acc. Depr. - Auto	0
Lawn Equipment	1,500
Acc. Depr. - Lawn Equipment	0
Accounts Payable	(2,000)
Notes payable	(8,000)
Interest Payable	0
Unearned Revenue	(360)
Capital	(3,000)
Drawing	0
Revenue	0
Landscaping Supplies Expense	0
Auto Expense	80
Advertising Expense	315
Equipment Rental Expense	75
Insurance Expense	0
Depreciation Expense - Auto	0
Depreciation Expense - Lawn E	0
Interest Expense	0
Total Debits - Total (credits)	0
Net Income	470

10) 7/16 Paid for a years' worth of general liability insurance for $1,000

Cash is affected and goes down with a credit. The second account must then be debited. The second account is prepaid insurance. Prepaid means it is an asset and not an expense. The reason we are recording to an asset and not an expense is that the insurance has not yet been used, or consumed, to help generate revenue. Assets have a normal debit balance and go up by doing the same thing of a debit.

7/16	Prepaid insurance	1,000	
	Cash-Checking		(1,000)

Transaction is then posted to the general ledger.

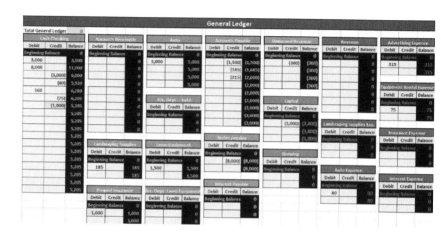

The trial balance is constructed from the general ledger. Note that the ending balances on the general ledger are what comprise the balances in the trial balance.

Accounts	Trial Balance
Cash-Checking	5,205
Accounts Receivable	0
Landscaping Supplies	185
Prepaid insurance	1,000
Auto	5,000
Acc. Depr. - Auto	0
Lawn Equipment	1,500
Acc. Depr. - Lawn Equipment	0
Accounts Payable	(2,000)
Notes payable	(8,000)
Interest Payable	0
Unearned Revenue	(360)
Capital	(3,000)
Drawing	0
Revenue	0
Landscaping Supplies Expense	0
Auto Expense	80
Advertising Expense	315
Equipment Rental Expense	75
Insurance Expense	0
Depreciation Expense - Auto	0
Depreciation Expense - Lawn E	0
Interest Expense	0
Total Debits - Total (credits)	0
Net Income	470

11) 7/17 completed a job and generated an invoice to be paid in the future for $720

Cash is not affected. An "I owe you" was received, a customer owing the company money for work completed. The "I owe you" account is accounts receivable, an asset, and is going up. Assets have normal debit balances and therefore will go up with a debit. The second account must then be credited. The second account is revenue. Revenue has a normal credit balance and will go up with a credit. Revenue generally

only goes up.

7/17	Accounts Receivable	720	
	Revenue		(720)

The transaction is then posted to the general ledger.

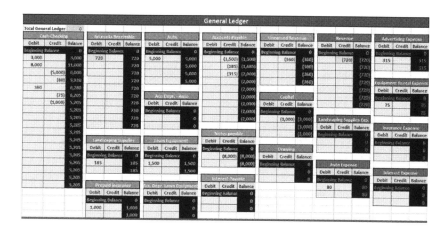

The trial balance is constructed from the general ledger. Note

that the ending balances on the general ledger are what comprise the

balances in the trial balance.

Accounts	Trial Balance
Cash-Checking	5,205
Accounts Receivable	720
Landscaping Supplies	185
Prepaid insurance	1,000
Auto	5,000
Acc. Depr. - Auto	0
Lawn Equipment	1,500
Acc. Depr. - Lawn Equipment	0
Accounts Payable	(2,000)
Notes payable	(8,000)
Interest Payable	0
Unearned Revenue	(360)
Capital	(3,000)
Drawing	0
Revenue	(720)
Landscaping Supplies Expense	0
Auto Expense	80
Advertising Expense	315
Equipment Rental Expense	75
Insurance Expense	0
Depreciation Expense - Auto	0
Depreciation Expense - Lawn E	0
Interest Expense	0
Total Debits - Total (credits)	0
Net Income	(250)

12) 7/18 purchase landscaping supplies on account for $140

Cash is not affected. Landscaping supplies were received.
Landscaping supplies is an asset. Assets have normal debit balances and
will go up with a debit. The second account must then be credited. The
second account is accounts payable. Accounts payable is a liability
account. Liability accounts have normal credit balances and go up with a
credit.

7/18	Landscaping Supplies	140	
	Accounts Payable		(140)

The transaction is then posted to the general ledger.

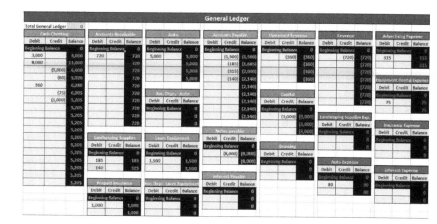

The trial balance is constructed from the general ledger. Note

that the ending balances on the general ledger are what comprise the

balances in the trial balance.

Accounts	Trial Balance
Cash-Checking	5,205
Accounts Receivable	720
Landscaping Supplies	325
Prepaid insurance	1,000
Auto	5,000
Acc. Depr. - Auto	0
Lawn Equipment	1,500
Acc. Depr. - Lawn Equipment	0
Accounts Payable	(2,140)
Notes payable	(8,000)
Interest Payable	0
Unearned Revenue	(360)
Capital	(3,000)
Drawing	0
Revenue	(720)
Landscaping Supplies Expense	0
Auto Expense	80
Advertising Expense	315
Equipment Rental Expense	75
Insurance Expense	0
Depreciation Expense - Auto	0
Depreciation Expense - Lawn E	0
Interest Expense	0
Total Debits - Total (credits)	0
Net Income	(250)

13) 7/20 completed a job and received partial payment of $250 of the invoiced amount of $550. $300 will be paid in the future.

Cash is affected and is going up by $250. This transaction is our first transaction that has more than two accounts affected. When work is completed we generally credit revenue, revenue having a normal credit balance and needing a credit to go up. Revenue should be credited for the total amount invoiced, the amount of the job of $550. An added debit of $300 will be needed for the journal entry to be in balance. The debit of $300 will go to the accounts receivable account, representing what is owed to the company. Accounts receivable is an

asset with a normal debit balance and a debit will make it go up.

7/20	Cash-Checking	250	
	Accounts Receivable	300	
	Revenue		(550)

The transaction is then posted to the general ledger.

The trial balance is constructed from the general ledger. Note

that the ending balances on the general ledger are what comprise the

balances in the trial balance.

Accounts	Trial Balance
Cash-Checking	5,455
Accounts Receivable	1,020
Landscaping Supplies	325
Prepaid insurance	1,000
Auto	5,000
Acc. Depr. - Auto	0
Lawn Equipment	1,500
Acc. Depr. - Lawn Equipment	0
Accounts Payable	(2,140)
Notes payable	(8,000)
Interest Payable	0
Unearned Revenue	(360)
Capital	(3,000)
Drawing	0
Revenue	(1,270)
Landscaping Supplies Expense	0
Auto Expense	80
Advertising Expense	315
Equipment Rental Expense	75
Insurance Expense	0
Depreciation Expense - Auto	0
Depreciation Expense - Lawn E	0
Interest Expense	0
Total Debits - Total (credits)	0
Net Income	(800)

14) 7/22 paid $175 for purchase made on account in the past

Cash is affected and is credited $175. The other account must then be debited. The second account is accounts payable. Accounts payable is a liability and must go down because the liability is being paid off. Accounts payable has a normal credit balance and is decreased with a debit.

7/22	Accounts Payable	175	
	Cash-Checking		(175)

The transaction is then posted to the general ledger.

General Ledger

Total General Ledger 0

Cash Checking

Debit	Credit	Balance
Beginning Balance		0
3,000		3,000
8,000		11,000
	(5,000)	6,000
	(80)	5,920
360		6,280
	(75)	6,205
	(1,000)	5,205
250		5,455
	(175)	5,280
		5,280
		5,280
		5,280
		5,280
		5,280
		5,280

Accounts Receivable

Debit	Credit	Balance
Beginning Balance		0
720		720
300		1,020
		1,020
		1,020
		1,020
		1,020
		1,020

Auto

Debit	Credit	Balance
Beginning Balance		0
5,000		5,000
		5,000
		5,000

Acc. Depr. Auto

Debit	Credit	Balance
Beginning Balance		0

Accounts Payable

Debit	Credit	Balance
Beginning Balance		0
	(1,500)	(1,500)
	(185)	(1,685)
	(315)	(2,000)
	(140)	(2,140)
175		(1,965)
		(1,965)
		(1,965)
		(1,815)
		(1,965)
		(1,965)

Notes Payable

Debit	Credit	Balance
Beginning Balance		0
	(8,000)	(8,000)
		(8,000)

Unearned Revenue

Debit	Credit	Balance
Beginning Balance		0
	(360)	(360)
		(360)
		(360)
		(360)

Capital

Debit	Credit	Balance
Beginning Balance		0
	(3,000)	(3,000)
		(3,000)

Drawing

Debit	Credit	Balance
Beginning Balance		0

Revenue

Debit	Credit	Balance
Beginning Balance		0
	(720)	(720)
	(550)	(1,270)
		(1,270)
		(1,270)
		(1,270)
		(1,270)

Landscaping Supplies Exp.

Debit	Credit	Balance
Beginning Balance		0

Auto Expense

Debit	Credit	Balance
Beginning Balance		0
80		80

Advertising Expense

Debit	Credit	Balance
Beginning Balance		0
315		315
		315

Equipment Rental Expense

Debit	Credit	Balance
Beginning Balance		0
75		75
		75

Insurance Expense

Debit	Credit	Balance
Beginning Balance		0
		0

Interest Expense

Debit	Credit	Balance
Beginning Balance		0
		0

Landscaping Supplies

Debit	Credit	Balance
Beginning Balance		0
185		185
140		325

Lawn Equipment

Debit	Credit	Balance
Beginning Balance		0
1,500		1,500
		1,560

Prepaid Insurance

Debit	Credit	Balance
Beginning Balance		0
1,000		1,000
		1,000

Acc. Depr. Lawn Equipment

Debit	Credit	Balance
Beginning Balance		0

Interest Payable

Debit	Credit	Balance
Beginning Balance		0

The trial balance is constructed from the general ledger. Note that the ending balances on the general ledger are what comprise the balances in the trial balance.

Accounts	Trial Balance
Cash-Checking	5,280
Accounts Receivable	1,020
Landscaping Supplies	325
Prepaid Insurance	1,000
Auto	5,000
Acc. Depr. - Auto	0
Lawn Equipment	1,500
Acc. Depr. - Lawn Equipment	0
Accounts Payable	(1,965)
Notes payable	(8,000)
Interest Payable	0
Unearned Revenue	(360)
Capital	(3,000)
Drawing	0
Revenue	(1,270)
Landscaping Supplies Expense	0
Auto Expense	80
Advertising Expense	315
Equipment Rental Expense	75
Insurance Expense	0
Depreciation Expense - Auto	0
Depreciation Expense - Lawn E	0
Interest Expense	0
Total Debits - Total (credits)	0
Net Income	(800)

15) 7/24 paid $40 for fuel and oil

Cash is affected and is going down with a credit. The other account must then be debited. The second account is auto expense. Expenses have a normal debit balance and go up with a debit.

7/24	Auto Expense	40	
	Cash-Checking		(40)

The transaction is then posted to the general ledger.

General Ledger

The trial balance is constructed from the general ledger. Note that the ending balances on the general ledger are what comprise the balances in the trial balance.

Accounts	Trial Balance
Cash-Checking	5,240
Accounts Receivable	1,020
Landscaping Supplies	325
Prepaid insurance	1,000
Auto	5,000
Acc. Depr. - Auto	0
Lawn Equipment	1,500
Acc. Depr. - Lawn Equipment	0
Accounts Payable	(1,965)
Notes payable	(8,000)
Interest Payable	0
Unearned Revenue	(360)
Capital	(3,000)
Drawing	0
Revenue	(1,270)
Landscaping Supplies Expense	0
Auto Expense	120
Advertising Expense	315
Equipment Rental Expense	75
Insurance Expense	0
Depreciation Expense - Auto	0
Depreciation Expense - Lawn E	0
Interest Expense	0
Total Debits - Total (credits)	0
Net Income	(760)

16) 7/24 completed a job on account and invoiced client $425.

Cash is not affected. An "I owe you" was received for work completed. Accounts receivable is an asset with a debit normal balance and will go up with a debit. The second account must then be credited. The second account will be revenue because work was done and revenue was earned.

7/24	Accounts Receivable	425	
	Revenue		(425)

The transaction is then posted to the general ledger.

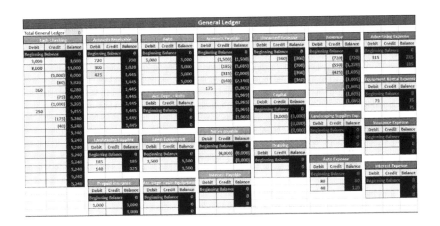

The trial balance is constructed from the general ledger. Note that the ending balances on the general ledger are what comprise the balances in the trial balance.

Accounts	Trial Balance
Cash-Checking	5,240
Accounts Receivable	1,445
Landscaping Supplies	325
Prepaid insurance	1,000
Auto	5,000
Acc. Depr. - Auto	0
Lawn Equipment	1,500
Acc. Depr. - Lawn Equipment	0
Accounts Payable	(1,965)
Notes payable	(8,000)
Interest Payable	0
Unearned Revenue	(360)
Capital	(3,000)
Drawing	0
Revenue	(1,695)
Landscaping Supplies Expense	0
Auto Expense	120
Advertising Expense	315
Equipment Rental Expense	75
Insurance Expense	0
Depreciation Expense - Auto	0
Depreciation Expense - Lawn E	0
Interest Expense	0
Total Debits - Total (credits)	0
Net Income	(1,185)

17) 7/26 completed a job on account and invoice client $150.

Cash is not affected. An "I owe you" was received for work

completed. Accounts receivable is an asset with a debit normal balance

and will go up with a debit. The second account must then be credited.

The second account will be revenue because work was done and revenue was earned.

7/26	Accounts Receivable	150	
	Revenue		(150)

The transaction is then posted to the general ledger.

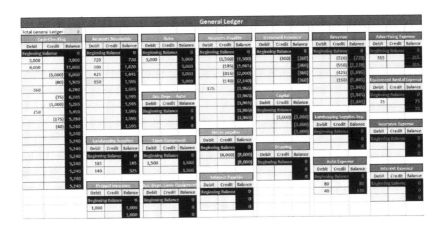

The trial balance is constructed from the general ledger. Note that the ending balances on the general ledger are what comprise the balances in the trial balance.

Accounts	Trial Balance
Cash-Checking	5,240
Accounts Receivable	1,595
Landscaping Supplies	325
Prepaid insurance	1,000
Auto	5,000
Acc. Depr. - Auto	0
Lawn Equipment	1,500
Acc. Depr. - Lawn Equipment	0
Accounts Payable	(1,965)
Notes payable	(8,000)
Interest Payable	0
Unearned Revenue	(360)
Capital	(3,000)
Drawing	0
Revenue	(1,845)
Landscaping Supplies Expense	0
Auto Expense	120
Advertising Expense	315
Equipment Rental Expense	75
Insurance Expense	0
Depreciation Expense - Auto	0
Depreciation Expense - Lawn E	0
Interest Expense	0
Total Debits - Total (credits)	0
Net Income	(1,335)

18) 7/26 received cash of $720 for work done in the past.

Cash is affected and goes up with a debit. The second account must then be credited. The second account is account receivable, an asset representing amounts owed to the business by customers. Accounts receivable has a normal debit balance and will go down with a credit.

7/26	Cash-Checking	720	
	Accounts Receivable		(720)

The transaction is then posted to the general ledger.

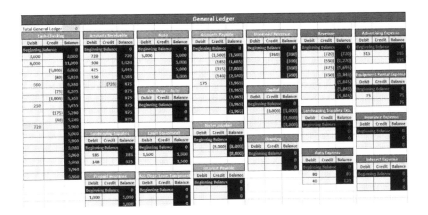

The trial balance is constructed from the general ledger. Note that the ending balances on the general ledger are what comprise the balances in the trial balance.

Accounts	Trial Balance
Cash-Checking	5,960
Accounts Receivable	875
Landscaping Supplies	325
Prepaid insurance	1,000
Auto	5,000
Acc. Depr. - Auto	0
Lawn Equipment	1,500
Acc. Depr. - Lawn Equipment	0
Accounts Payable	(1,965)
Notes payable	(8,000)
Interest Payable	0
Unearned Revenue	(360)
Capital	(3,000)
Drawing	0
Revenue	(1,845)
Landscaping Supplies Expense	0
Auto Expense	120
Advertising Expense	315
Equipment Rental Expense	75
Insurance Expense	0
Depreciation Expense - Auto	0
Depreciation Expense - Lawn E	0
Interest Expense	0
Total Debits - Total (credits)	0
Net Income	(1,335)

19) 7/27 completed a job and received partial payment of $200 of $700, the customer still owing $500 in the future.

Cash is affected and is going up by $200. This transaction is one of the few journal entries we are working with that has more than two accounts. Because we completed a job the second account, the one credited, will be revenue. Revenue has a normal balance of a credit and always goes up in the credit direction. Revenue will be credited for $700, the amount of the invoice. The difference of a debit of $500 needed to balance the journal entry will go to accounts receivable

representing that the customer owes the business.

7/27	Cash-Checking	200	
	Accounts Receivable	500	
	Revenue		(700)

The transaction is then posted to the general ledger.

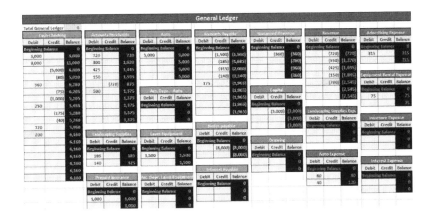

The trial balance is constructed from the general ledger. Note

that the ending balances on the general ledger are what comprise the

balances in the trial balance.

Accounts	Trial Balance
Cash-Checking	6,160
Accounts Receivable	1,375
Landscaping Supplies	325
Prepaid insurance	1,000
Auto	5,000
Acc. Depr. - Auto	0
Lawn Equipment	1,500
Acc. Depr. - Lawn Equipment	0
Accounts Payable	(1,965)
Notes payable	(8,000)
Interest Payable	0
Unearned Revenue	(360)
Capital	(3,000)
Drawing	0
Revenue	(2,545)
Landscaping Supplies Expense	0
Auto Expense	120
Advertising Expense	315
Equipment Rental Expense	75
Insurance Expense	0
Depreciation Expense - Auto	0
Depreciation Expense - Lawn E	0
Interest Expense	0
Total Debits - Total (credits)	0
Net Income	(2,035)

20) 7/27 received cash of $150 for work done in the past.

Cash is affected and will go up by $150. The second account must then be credited by $150. The second account is account receivable, an asset representing money owed from customers, which must go down. Accounts receivable has a normal debit balance and a credit will make it go down.

7/27	Cash-Checking	150	
	Accounts Receivable		(150)

The transaction is then posted to the general ledger.

General Ledger

| Total General Ledger | 0 | | | | | | | | | | | | | | | | | | | | |

Cash-Checking

Debit	Credit	Balance
Beginning Balance		0
5,000		3,000
8,000		11,000
	(5,000)	6,000
	(80)	5,920
360		6,280
	(75)	6,205
	(1,000)	5,205
250		5,455
	(175)	5,280
	(40)	5,240
720		5,960
200		6,160
150		6,310
		6,310
		6,310
		6,310
		6,310

Accounts Receivable

Debit	Credit	Balance
Beginning Balance		0
720		720
300		1,020
425		1,445
150		1,595
	(720)	875
500		1,375
	(150)	1,225
		1,225
		1,225
		1,225

Accum Depr - Auto

Debit	Credit	Balance
Beginning Balance		0
		0

Landscaping Supplies

Debit	Credit	Balance
Beginning Balance		0
185		185
140		325

Prepaid Insurance

Debit	Credit	Balance
Beginning Balance		0
1,000		1,000
		1,000

Debit	Credit	Balance
Beginning Balance		0
5,000		5,000
		5,000
		5,000
		5,000

Auto & Equipment

Debit	Credit	Balance
Beginning Balance		0
1,500		1,500
		1,500

Acc Depr - Lawn Equipment

Debit	Credit	Balance
Beginning Balance		0

Deferred Revenue

Debit	Credit	Balance
Beginning Balance		0
	(1,500)	(1,500)
	(185)	(1,685)
	(315)	(2,000)
	(140)	(2,140)
175		(1,965)
		(1,965)
		(1,965)
		(1,965)
		(1,965)

Wages payable

Debit	Credit	Balance
Beginning Balance		0

Interest Payable

Debit	Credit	Balance
Beginning Balance		0

Deferred Revenue

Debit	Credit	Balance
Beginning Balance		0
	(360)	(360)
		(360)
		(360)
		(360)

Capital

Debit	Credit	Balance
Beginning Balance		0
	(8,000)	(8,000)
		(8,000)

Drawing

Debit	Credit	Balance
Beginning Balance		0
0		0

Revenue

Debit	Credit	Balance
Beginning Balance		0
	(720)	(720)
	(550)	(1,270)
	(425)	(1,695)
	(150)	(1,845)
	(700)	(2,545)
		(2,545)
		(2,545)

Landscaping Supplies Exp.

Debit	Credit	Balance
Beginning Balance		0

Auto Expense

Debit	Credit	Balance
Beginning Balance		0

Advertising Expense

Debit	Credit	Balance
Beginning Balance		0
315		315
		315

Equipment Rental Expense

Debit	Credit	Balance
Beginning Balance		0
75		75
		75

Insurance Expense

Debit	Credit	Balance
Beginning Balance		0

Interest Expense

Debit	Credit	Balance
Beginning Balance		0
80		80
40		120

The trial balance is constructed from the general ledger. Note that the ending balances on the general ledger are what comprise the balances in the trial balance.

Accounts	Trial Balance
Cash-Checking	6,310
Accounts Receivable	1,225
Landscaping Supplies	325
Prepaid insurance	1,000
Auto	5,000
Acc. Depr. - Auto	0
Lawn Equipment	1,500
Acc. Depr. - Lawn Equipment	0
Accounts Payable	(1,965)
Notes payable	(8,000)
Interest Payable	0
Unearned Revenue	(360)
Capital	(3,000)
Drawing	0
Revenue	(2,545)
Landscaping Supplies Expense	0
Auto Expense	120
Advertising Expense	315
Equipment Rental Expense	75
Insurance Expense	0
Depreciation Expense - Auto	0
Depreciation Expense - Lawn E	0
Interest Expense	0
Total Debits - Total (credits)	0
Net Income	(2,035)

21) 7/28 paid $75 for a purchase made in the past on account.

Cash is affected and goes down with a credit. The second account must then be a debit. The second account is accounts payable, a liability account representing what the business owes, and it must go down. Accounts payable has a normal credit balance and will go down with a debit.

7/28	Accounts Payable	75	
	Cash-Checking		(75)

The transaction is then posted to the general ledger.

General Ledger

The trial balance is constructed from the general ledger. Note that the ending balances on the general ledger are what comprise the balances in the trial balance.

Accounts	Trial Balance
Cash-Checking	6,235
Accounts Receivable	1,225
Landscaping Supplies	325
Prepaid insurance	1,000
Auto	5,000
Acc. Depr. - Auto	0
Lawn Equipment	1,500
Acc. Depr. - Lawn Equipment	0
Accounts Payable	(1,890)
Notes payable	(8,000)
Interest Payable	0
Unearned Revenue	(360)
Capital	(3,000)
Drawing	0
Revenue	(2,545)
Landscaping Supplies Expense	0
Auto Expense	120
Advertising Expense	315
Equipment Rental Expense	75
Insurance Expense	0
Depreciation Expense - Auto	0
Depreciation Expense - Lawn E	0
Interest Expense	0
Total Debits - Total (credits)	0
Net Income	(2,035)

22) 7/30 received $425 cash for work done in the past.

Cash is affected and goes up with a debit. The second account must then be credited. The second account is accounts receivable, an asset account that needs to go down. Accounts receivable has a normal debit balance and goes down with a credit.

7/30	Cash-Checking	425	
	Accounts Receivable		(425)

The transaction is then posted to the general ledger.

General Ledger

The trial balance is constructed from the general ledger. Note that the ending balances on the general ledger are what comprise the balances in the trial balance.

Accounts	Trial Balance
Cash-Checking	6,660
Accounts Receivable	800
Landscaping Supplies	325
Prepaid insurance	1,000
Auto	5,000
Acc. Depr. - Auto	0
Lawn Equipment	1,500
Acc. Depr. - Lawn Equipment	0
Accounts Payable	(1,890)
Notes payable	(8,000)
Interest Payable	0
Unearned Revenue	(360)
Capital	(3,000)
Drawing	0
Revenue	(2,545)
Landscaping Supplies Expense	0
Auto Expense	120
Advertising Expense	315
Equipment Rental Expense	75
Insurance Expense	0
Depreciation Expense - Auto	0
Depreciation Expense - Lawn E	0
Interest Expense	0
Total Debits - Total (credits)	0
Net Income	(2,035)

23) 7/30 owner withdraws cash for personal use of $500.

Cash is affected and goes down with a credit. The second account must then be a debit. The second account is called drawings and is an equity account representing withdrawals, usually in cash, by the owner. Drawing is a temporary account but not an income statement account. The drawings account is an equity account but the account has a debit balance. The drawings account goes up with debits. When drawing increases total equity decreases.

7/30	Drawing		500	
	Cash-Checking			(500)

The transaction is then posted to the general ledger.

General Ledger

The trial balance is constructed from the general ledger. Note that the ending balances on the general ledger are what comprise the balances in the trial balance.

Accounts	Trial Balance
Cash-Checking	6,160
Accounts Receivable	800
Landscaping Supplies	325
Prepaid insurance	1,000
Auto	5,000
Acc. Depr. - Auto	0
Lawn Equipment	1,500
Acc. Depr. - Lawn Equipment	0
Accounts Payable	(1,890)
Notes payable	(8,000)
Interest Payable	0
Unearned Revenue	(360)
Capital	(3,000)
Drawing	500
Revenue	(2,545)
Landscaping Supplies Expense	0
Auto Expense	120
Advertising Expense	315
Equipment Rental Expense	75
Insurance Expense	0
Depreciation Expense - Auto	0
Depreciation Expense - Lawn E	0
Interest Expense	0
Total Debits - Total (credits)	0
Net Income	(2,035)

Glossary (John J. Wild, 2015) Click here for videos

Account – Record within an accounting system in which increases and decreases are entered and stored in a specific asset, liability, equity, revenue, or expense.

Account balance – Difference between total debits and total credits (including the beginning balance) for an account.

Chart of accounts – List of accounts used by a company; includes an identification number for each account.

Credit – Recorded on the right side; an entry that decreases asset and expense accounts, and increases liability, revenue, and equity accounts.

Creditors – Individuals or organizations entitled to receive payments.

Debit – Recorded on the left side; an entry that increases assets and expense accounts, and decreases liability, revenue, and equity accounts.

Double entry accounting – Accounting system in which each transaction affects at least two accounts and has at least one debit and one credit.

General journal – All-purpose journal for recording the debits and credits of transactions and events.

General Ledger – Record containing all accounts (with amounts) for a business; also called ledger.

Journal – Record in which transactions are entered before they are posted to ledger accounts; also called book of original entry.

Journalizing – Process of recording transactions in a journal.

Posting – Process of transferring journal entry information to the ledger; computerized systems automate this process.

T-account – Tool used to show the effects of transactions and events on individual accounts.

Trial Balance – List of accounts and their balances at a point in time; total debit balances equal total credit balances.

Unearned revenue – Liability created when customers pay in advance for products or services; earned when the products or services are later delivered.

References

AICPA. (n.d.). *AICPA.org*. Retrieved from AICPA.org:
https://www.aicpa.org/About/FAQs/Pages/default.aspx#aicpa_
answer13

John J. Wild, K. W. (2015). *Fundamental Accounting Principles 22e.*
McGraw-Hill Education.